Vulnerable and Free

An encouragement for those sharing in the life of Jesus

Fr. Paul Farren

Foreword by Timothy Shriver

PARACLETE PRESS
BREWSTER, MASSACHUSETTS

2019 First Printing

Vulnerable and Free: An Encouragement for Those Sharing in the Life of Jesus

Copyright © 2019 by Paul Farren

ISBN 978-1-64060-200-7

All quotations from Scripture use the translation of The Jerusalem Bible, published by Darton, Longman, & Todd Ltd., London, 1974. Used by permission.

The Paraclete Press name and logo (dove on cross) are trademarks of Paraclete Press, Inc.

Library of Congress Cataloging-in-Publication Data
Names: Farren, Paul (Catholic priest), author.
Title: Vulnerable and free : an encouragement for those sharing in the life
   of Jesus / Farren Paul ; foreword by Tim Shriver .
Description: Brewster, MA : Paraclete Press, Inc., 2019.
Identifiers: LCCN 2019014685 | ISBN 9781640602007 (tradepaper)
Subjects: LCSH: Personality—Religious aspects—Christianity. |
   Vulnerability (Personality trait) | Consolation. | Sufferin—Religious
   aspects—Christianity. | Success—Religious aspects—Christianity.
Classification: LCC BV4597.57 .F37 2019 | DDC 248.8/6—dc23
LC record available at https://lccn.loc.gov/2019014685

10 9 8 7 6 5 4 3 2 1

All rights reserved. No portion of this book may be reproduced, stored in an electronic retrieval system, or transmitted in any form or by any means—electronic, mechanical, photocopy, recording, or any other—except for brief quotations in printed reviews, without the prior permission of the publisher.

Published by Paraclete Press
Brewster, Massachusetts
www.paracletepress.com
Printed in the United States of America

IN MEMORY *of* Jean Vanier

Contents

Foreword	by Timothy Shriver	7
Introduction	***This Is Our Story***	13
One	***Vulnerable and Free***	19
Two	***From Competition to Communion***	37
Three	***From the Need for Power to Discovering Poverty as a Place of Love***	55
Four	***From Humiliation to Acceptance of Who We Really Are***	71
Five	***Fruits from Humiliation***	85
Six	***All Things Pass Away***	97
Seven	***Death***	111
Eight	***For the Road Home***	127
Conclusion		135
Afterword		141

Foreword

*P*erhaps nothing could be more important to the world today than an honest and raw exploration of the deceptions and allure of power.

In my own career, I've been a part of countless conversations about power. In schools around the world, I and many of my fellow educators are trying to "empower" young people by teaching them agency and grit. In companies around the world, I've joined with business leaders who seek the power to win in a competitive marketplace. In families around the world, and in my own, women and men are trying to find new ways to share power and balance power and celebrate each other's power. These conversations are almost invariably seen as a source of progress and newness. Power is good. Finding new ways to get it and use it and occasionally share it is essential.

And then I read Paul Farren's book, *Vulnerable and Free*, and my heart was caught off guard by a wise and heart-opening reflection on the transformative, if often unwelcome, power of powerlessness. And all of a sudden, powerlessness became alluring! In this beautiful book, Fr. Farren carries us along in search of a more lasting power, and in these pages, we find it. Start almost anywhere in this book, and the world is turned inside out. My heart was cracked open reading of the powerlessness Jeffrey felt in the repeated abandonment and abuse he experienced at the hand of his father. But then this same young man was able to forgive his dad and care for him in the hospital with tenderness and compassion. As I felt both Jeffrey's pain and transcendent strength, I was led to wonder, How does he do that? How does he still love his dad? Forgiveness is a gift, it seems, from a higher power. And forgiveness is its own power that, despite how much pain it takes to find it, is the key to being freed from a past that so often haunts and binds us.

I was stunned by yet another story in the book—the account of Christian de Chergé, the prior of the Monastery of Our Lady of Atlas in Algeria. When violence and terror were sweeping their country, Fr. Christian and his fellow monks refused to leave even as the risk of their murder grew overwhelming, even as they knew of their very likely deaths. I wondered about the fear, the helplessness, the powerlessness of those final days—about how they endured their final hours when the attackers arrived. And then I read Prior Christian's letter, written in anticipation of meeting his murderer, and I was reduced to tears: "And you also," Fr. Christian wrote, "the friend of my final moment, who would not be aware of what you were doing. Yes, for you also I wish this 'thank you'—and this adieu—to commend you to the God whose face I see in yours." Was Fr. Christian powerless? Perhaps. But his is a power I hunger to have.

The honest truth is that powerlessness and vulnerability are almost always unwelcome. And too frequently, they lead to a bitter descent into anger and shame and isolation. Is there a reader who has not taken that journey? I doubt it. Is there a reader who would want it? Surely not. At least, surely not me.

I have seen vulnerability and shame over and over again in my own life with people with intellectual differences. Their arrival is almost always a shock, a disruption, a time of grief. Parents long for the child they thought they would have. Siblings struggle to understand the brother or sister who is different. The messages from all around society lead to a kind of vortex of inescapable disappointment. We had hoped for a certain child. Instead, we have this child.

But there, in the very concrete and sometimes foggy moment, we come to see not any child, not a generic child, but *this* particular little boy or girl—her eyes, his toes, this child in my arms, gentle, longing for love, helplessly beautiful. And all the power that had once seemed so necessary fades away, and a different power breaks through. This child learns to crawl. This child starts to smile. This child holds your hand. And this child, who is so quickly dismissed as being powerless, begins to teach us all the freedom, the forgiveness, the irrefutable power of love.

In the end, of course, Fr. Farren isn't inviting us to be doormats for the world, powerless in a way that invites humiliation or despair. He is teaching us the lessons of the poor, powerless Savior of the world, who invites us into his own subversive and transformative power—the power to be free from fear, free from judgment, free from the illusions of death. His is a different type of power. It is power with and not power over. It is power shared, not power taken. It is power given, not power held. It is the raw and striking power of the truth that love is the energy of the universe—nothing more and nothing less. It is our source and our destiny too. It is always ours for the taking. It is the power that lasts.

In our time, the churches that many of us once saw as powerful are finding themselves brought low. Governments that many of us once saw as honorable are finding themselves humbled by glaring hypocrisy. So many people whom we once called "powerful" have been exposed as fraught, broken, and hiding. These can be sobering and discouraging times.

But in these pages, one finds no despair. Let the church rebuild herself on the energies of love alone and unleash a new era of believers guided only by that power. Let governments rebuild themselves with justice and joy and unleash a new era of citizens dedicated only to those gifts. Let the powerful meet and break bread with the powerless and find each other awash with peace and security and belonging. This is the promise of living vulnerable and free. It is as old as the Cross but ever subversive, ever new, ever needing us to let it break through.

In short, in these times of change and disruption, we need to each find our way to being converted, not to a particular creed, but to living vulnerable and free. This beautiful book has reminded me of both the difficulty and the hope of that search in my own life. For all of us, it is a good place to start the journey. For the world, we can't start soon enough.

Timothy Shriver, PhD, Chairman of Special Olympics, and author of *Fully Alive: Discovering What Matters Most*

Introduction
This Is Our Story

On June 15, 1946, Margaret Mary Coll was born in Portsalon, a small seaside town in the very north of Ireland in County Donegal. Margaret grew up there, and after finishing her schooling she went to Dublin to study to be a teacher. When she graduated, she returned to Donegal to begin her teaching career. She married and had two children. I was her second child, born in 1972.

In 1989, at the age of seventeen, I entered seminary to begin my studies for priesthood. I was one of the youngest students in the seminary. At the age of forty-three my mother was one of the youngest parents with a child in seminary. At family celebrations, I often looked around at the other mothers present and was so grateful that my mother was so young! I had a real sense that she would be with me for many years of priesthood. I felt so blessed.

Then in 1994 my mother was diagnosed with cancer. We were told that it wasn't too serious and that it was very curable. This gave my family confidence. However, the cancer didn't seem to ever loosen its grip on my mother. After each operation or course of treatment, it kept reappearing. I was to be ordained a deacon at the beginning of June 1995. My mother's health was weakening, and her doctor told me that she probably wouldn't live until then. I contacted my bishop, who changed the date of my ordination to the diaconate to May. My mother was quite weak at that time, but she was there. It was the last Mass that she attended. My mother died June 4, 1995, eleven days before her forty-ninth birthday.

It was all wrong and unnatural and too fast. As my mother was preparing to die, I was discerning my call to be ordained. There seemed to be so many contradictions in what was happening. One was choosing for life. The other was preparing for death. So I could have asked the question, Since all life ends in death anyway, what was the point in taking a road of celibacy and service? And then, Since all life ends in death, would it not be better to try to find a path that would have the potential to bring me surer happiness—a life that avoided sacrifice, or at least understood that all forms of self-renunciation was a waste of time since time could be short? What is the sense in priesthood—in many ways an incomplete life—if death can wield its power at any time? Would it not be better to achieve everything in this world? Would it not be wiser to try to find complete fulfillment when I still had the time—fulfillment in this world? These were lonely questions.

While I do not believe that God creates occasions of suffering for us, I do believe that God can teach us through our experience of suffering. What I learned at that time was, rather than it making no sense to be ordained a priest in the context of death, it only made sense to be ordained a priest in the context of death! In the context of this world only, priesthood is at best absurd and celibacy is nonsense. We need the context of eternal life to live many of the experiences of this life. My mother's death revealed the incompleteness that is often to be found in this life. If we look for completeness in this world, we will never find it. It is simply not possible.

This book as it charts the journey of life—not just my experiences, but *any* human life—will examine how we can face and live the incompleteness of our time on earth, including the failures of our lives, with hope and confidence.

The journey of this life is one that begins with complete dependency before and after birth. These times are times of great vulnerability. Then, as we begin to make our way in this world, we try to overcome our dependency and vulnerability. In many ways, we begin to strive for independence, for control, for power. Strength and self-sufficiency then can become the acceptable goals in life, and dependency and vulnerability are often seen as only negative realities to be avoided or denied at all costs.

But independence, control, and power cannot last forever. The journey of life seems to inevitably lead us on to new places of dependency and vulnerability—which are perhaps more accurately described as places of poverty. Without doubt, we view these as very undesirable places in which to be.

We don't want to be poor. We don't want to be in need. We don't want to be weak. With all these realities—with poverty—there comes humiliation. We dread humiliation. We are humiliated when our poverty becomes public—when our need is laid bare for others to see. In that place of humiliation, we seem to be completely powerless.

But the power we have in humiliation is the power to decide. We have the power to decide how we react to our humiliation. Do we react to it in anger? Do we react to it in shame? If we choose either of these, we are led to a place of paralysis. We become paralyzed by our anger or by our shame. We become consumed with them. When this happens, it can only lead to death even if we are still alive. We do not have the energy to live if we are consumed by the anger and shame that can come from our humiliation. These emotions can take over our lives. Then we become bitter.

There is no life in bitterness. However, it doesn't have to be this way.

There is another way. It is the way of freedom that comes from self-acceptance and the acceptance of the reality that we are faced with. In order to choose the way of freedom, we need to be reflective—to be open to the revelation of God in prayer and through others. This is a real challenge and takes great strength, but it is possible. It is necessary, too, because freedom only comes from truth, and truth is the acceptance of reality. When we have the courage to accept reality, we are free to live in that reality but not be held captive by it. This freedom enables us to see beyond ourselves. It puts our life into a bigger context. It reveals to us what truly matters and enables us to love and allows us to be loved. This really is a journey from vulnerability back to vulnerability. Along the way we discover what matters and what lasts. We also discover what passes away.

This book takes you on that journey. This book is really about a journey home. And while on the way home, we will put death in its proper place!

One
Vulnerable and Free

There have been so many terrorist attacks in the world in the last few years. I recall the truck that was driven indiscriminately into a large group of people who were celebrating Bastille Day in Nice, France, on July 14, 2016. More than eighty people were killed. There are so many attacks I could recall.

People are divided. People are afraid. People are becoming more and more defensive. Racism has risen dramatically. There is an *us* and a *them*—the native and the foreigner. Keep the foreigners out, send them home, are growing attitudes in many places today. Build walls. Erect barricades. Protect ourselves.

In the referendum in the United Kingdom about leaving the European Union, many people who voted in favor of leaving did so in the belief that, by leaving, the foreigners would be sent home. They would get their country back for themselves. They look forward to mass deportations.

A couple of weeks after the referendum, the Gospel for the Sunday was the story of the good Samaritan. Who is my neighbor? That Sunday I preached about racism and our attitude to those we call foreigners. I said that we tend to think and act in such a way that neighbors are fine—when they stay at home. It is when neighbors start coming into our houses that the problems can begin! We know the phrase "good fences make good neighbors." So the implication is that bad fences make bad neighbors. Maybe that is the problem in the world today. There are bad fences. If everybody stayed at home, things would be much, much better. If everybody stayed in their own country, there would be less trouble.

I was preaching in Derry, Northern Ireland—a place, as you may know, that has seen its share of troubles.

"Send the foreigners home," so many people seem to be saying just now. As I reminded my congregation, this is certainly no attitude for the Irish, because so many of us have been strangers in a foreign land. It was money made by Irish immigrants that enabled many Irish people to survive in their native land.

It can feel easy to love your neighbor—if they stay away from you. It can even be easy to give money to your neighbor—if you don't have to meet them or form a relationship with them. Send the money to Africa, but keep the Africans over there where they most belong. What happens when they come here? What happens when people from Eastern Europe come here? People become upset.

Sometimes we have the attitude that they are coming into our country as if we own this place where we are, and as if we have a divine right to whatever we want from it. Everything here is ours and we will only give a bit away if we have more than we want.

In the tenth chapter of the Gospel of Luke (see Lk. 10:25–37), we have a fascinating scenario. A man has been attacked. He has been left for dead. The leaders of society walk past him. They don't get involved. It is messy to get involved. Then the outcast comes—the foreigner. He suddenly and inexplicably gets involved. He uses his own resources to care for him. Why would he do this?

The foreigner and stranger places the man who was left for dead onto his own mount and brings him to an inn. He pays the innkeeper to care for him, and he commits to come back to see how he is doing, and to cover any expenses.

Who is my neighbor? Jesus tells us very directly and without any ambiguity who our neighbor is. Our neighbor is anybody and everybody in need. This is radical and not a pleasant Gospel in the climate that we are living in today. Jesus doesn't agree with good fences making good neighbors.

Good neighbors are people who will care for others at significant cost and upset to themselves. Good neighbors don't mark out their territory and claim rights to the detriment of others. Good neighbors are people who engage with others—who help others—who care for others. Good neighbors are people who take down fences and walls and barricades and welcome others and share with them.

If we are Christians and take the Gospel of Jesus seriously, we must admit that we have no right to tell anybody to go home. We don't own this land or its resources. We don't have any exclusive rights to anything. We are here by an accident of birth, and everybody and anybody who comes here for whatever reason is our sister or our brother. We are called to care for them and love them and be grateful to God for them. If truth be told, we are all foreigners in this world because our true home is in heaven.

In the Gospel story from Luke, the lawyer asks Jesus what he has to do to inherit eternal life. The answer he is given is very simple: love. The evidence that we want to go to heaven will be found in how much we actively and truly love here on earth.

After Mass that day, after I had preached that sermon, as I stood at the door greeting people as they exited, I had two interesting encounters.

The first encounter was with two young men, probably in their twenties. They were brothers. One said to me, "I agree in principle with most of what you said, but . . ." His *but* was around the issue of patriotism. He believed that we did indeed have ownership of our country; it is ours by right. He also seemed to have a strong sense that we were the chosen people to the detriment of others and therefore deserved superior treatment. To make his point, he referred to another story from the Gospel in which Jesus encounters a woman who asks for the scraps that fall from the Master's table (see Matt. 15:21–28). I suggested that, if you look closely at that other story, the woman ends up getting a lot more than scraps from Jesus. The patriotic-feeling brothers were unconvinced, and they went away unhappy with me. It was a disquieting encounter that moved neither of us toward the other.

Then, as I went back into the church, there was another man waiting for me. This man is from Africa.

He shook my hand and thanked me for saying what I said. He said that it made him feel so welcome in our community.

As I reflected later on these two encounters, I became so aware of the vulnerability of the man from Africa. He had, for whatever reason, left all that he was familiar with to come to Derry. He left his native home and came to a foreign place where he is at the mercy of those in that place. They have the power to make him feel welcome or to reject him. His vulnerability was so obvious even in the manner in which he approached me. He waited for me quietly at the back of the church, after others had had their say and headed for home. He was so humble as he stretched out his hand to me.

The place of vulnerability is a dangerous place. It is a place of need, a place of openness, a place of weakness. When we are vulnerable, we are dependent on the actions of others. When we are vulnerable, we cannot pretend to be independent. Our vulnerability reveals our dependency. That is dangerous because our need may not be met. Then we can feel rejected, abandoned. We can feel inferior. We can feel afraid. Therefore, the place of vulnerability is rarely a place we want to be in for long. It is a place we desire to leave rather than arrive in. We want to leave our vulnerability behind, our weakness behind, our need behind. We can see this so often in our lives.

Our very entry into this world is defined by vulnerability. Think of it. During our nine months in the womb, we are completely dependent on our mother. It is her body that enables us to grow. Without the umbilical cord, we are starved. Without the protection of the womb, we die. Sadly, for too many of us the profound danger of our vulnerability is laid bare when our time in the womb of our mother is cut short through abortion. Our vulnerability can also be terribly exploited when our mother takes drugs or alcohol while we are in her womb. I know a couple who adopted a child whose mother was addicted to drugs. It was so painful for them to watch their child in the early months of his life fighting the illnesses that he suffered as a result of his mother's addictions. Being vulnerable is dangerous.

At the moment of birth in many ways our vulnerability is made public. Many more people see our vulnerability. Unlike so many other mammals, the human baby is totally dependent for everything. The baby's need is all-encompassing. This little human being can do virtually nothing on his or her own. This is complete vulnerability and dependence.

Then as the baby develops, moments of independence are celebrated—the first step taken unaided. The child is naturally encouraged to become more and more independent. Most children love this, and they want to show their independence. "I can do it on my own" can become a defensive mantra when the child rejects help. The vulnerability seems to decrease. As we become more independent, we tend to feel less vulnerable. Yet the transition from childhood into adulthood is not simply a transition from vulnerability to independence. It is not that simple.

Vulnerability seems to follow us wherever we go, although sometimes we try not to acknowledge the reality.

The child can become quite independent at home in many ways, and then when they step out of home and go to school, it can all change again. They can feel they are the boss at home, but when they go to school, they can feel that they are a very little person again. They become vulnerable in this big place full of people—many of them strangers. Then they can get over that vulnerability, but they can't stay at that school forever, and so they start all over again seven or eight years later in a new and often bigger school. They are vulnerable again. Even in school, new classes and new subjects make us vulnerable. When we are learning sports or musical instruments, we are vulnerable. Often, we react to this vulnerability. We don't like being in vulnerable places.

I know, from my own life, that I hated learning to drive. My father taught me, and he was a very good teacher, but I hated the feeling of need and weakness. In hindsight, my father was an awful lot more vulnerable than me in the process!

So we continue to be vulnerable. A new job, a new place of work—in these realities we need help. We need to learn. In relationships, too, we are vulnerable. As we enter a new relationship, we open ourselves to the other, and we always run the risk that we might be rejected. We might be abandoned. Most of us struggle with this reality. Sometimes even in marriage after many faithful years a spouse can leave—walk out often to another relationship. This can cause a terrible feeling of abandonment and rejection for the spouse left behind. In the recent past with all the financial instability and crash, many people became bankrupt. They had to start working all over again, realizing how vulnerable they were. They too were often rejected by people and institutions that once supported and encouraged them. It is very difficult. It is so painful—searing pain.

Then we have the ultimate vulnerability. This is the vulnerability that ill health and age brings. This is a vulnerability that increases and increases until we die.

The dying process for many people is a process that leads them in a way of increased dependency. As their body weakens, their need continues to grow. The need grows to a moment when it cannot be met in any way. That is the moment of return. It is the moment that we return to the One who made us.

We enter this world as completely vulnerable human beings, and we leave this world in the exact same way. In many ways, it is the completion of the circle. At the beginning, we are unable to do anything for ourselves. At the end, it is often the same. We remember how, after Jesus commissioned Peter to go out and feed his lambs, to feed his sheep, Jesus also gave Peter a glimpse of the future. It wasn't a future of fat lambs and fat sheep. Jesus said:

> I tell you most solemnly, when you were young you put on your own belt and walked where you liked; but when you grow old you will stretch out your hands, and somebody else will put a belt round you and take you where you would rather not go. (John 21:18)

This doesn't seem to be such a great motivational speech by Jesus to Peter! He was sending him out to be nourishment for others. He was sending him out as a leader. A picture of the future that might have enthused Peter a bit more would have been one with many followers listening to his word. Yet Jesus showed him a future where he wouldn't be able to dress himself and he wouldn't have the freedom to decide where he wanted to go. It was a future of weakness, maybe even humiliation. This appears to be a very grim future—a future to be avoided. It certainly doesn't appear to be a future to be embraced. Was Jesus revealing to Peter that ultimately he would be a failure? Nobody wants to end life unable to dress themselves. Nobody wants to end life not being able to make their own decisions. They find it humiliating.

There are so many examples of this journey to weakness—to vulnerability in life. Some of them are very public.

A number of years ago, there was a very powerful photograph published of Margaret Thatcher, the former

British prime minister. It was toward the end of her life, and she was in a park in London. She appeared extremely frail and was being guided and helped by a carer. This was the woman whom we once knew as the Iron Lady—the most powerful woman in the world. She had gone from a place of great power to a place of profound vulnerability.

We arrive in the world into a place of vulnerability, but it is a place we try to leave as quickly as possible. However, in all our efforts to leave the place of vulnerability, we arrive back at it, and it is from there that we do leave the world. We leave this world from a place of the most radical vulnerability. For that reason, we are very justified in asking the question, Does all human life end in failure? We desire so much to be independent, and yet, ultimately, we fail spectacularly because we die.

So what do we do with all of this vulnerability in our lives? We cannot ignore it, because it will catch up with

Vulnerable and Free   33

us. There seems to be no escape from it. We spend our lives trying to get away from it, but ultimately it always seems to catch us. So what do we do?

The most amazing reality in the story of God is that it is all about vulnerability. God is all-powerful and all-knowing. God is completely independent and needs nothing. Yet when God entered this world, he embraced vulnerability. God didn't enter the world as an all-powerful warrior who would take control of the world. God could enter the world any way that he wanted. God chose to enter the world as a vulnerable little baby. This is the most amazing reality. Surely God shouldn't be a vulnerable baby. It seems to make absolutely no sense. Yet God chose to be dependent on humanity.

He chose to be dependent on Mary when he sent the angel Gabriel to ask her to be the mother of his Son. Mary could have said no. God was vulnerable.

Then, in the birth of Jesus, the vulnerability of God became instantly even more apparent. Jesus was born as a homeless person. He was completely dependent on Mary and Joseph. While the shepherds and the wise men came to pay homage to him, Mary had to feed him and clean him.

After being homeless, the next title that Jesus earned was *refugee*. After Mary and Joseph and Jesus left Bethlehem, they went as refugees to Egypt. They were strangers in a foreign land. Our God was homeless and a refugee. Our God was dependent and in need.

At many times in the life of Jesus, he was vulnerable. He opened himself. He opened himself to rejection, and at times he was rejected. His vulnerability was dangerous.

His greatest moment of vulnerability was his passion and death. He was vulnerable to the actions of Judas, and this is clearly illustrated when Jesus says to Judas, "What you are going to do, do quickly" (John 13:27).

Jesus was so vulnerable in the garden of Gethsemane. He needed his friends, and they let him down. He felt abandoned. He was rejected. He was betrayed. He felt himself open, and he suffered so much as a result. After Gethsemane, the vulnerability increased.

The walk to Calvary was the walk of humiliation. Jesus was defeated, and he was made a spectacle of as he walked with this cross to his place of death. Jesus was utterly vulnerable as he dragged his weakening body to his place of death. The crucifixion of Jesus was the fruit of his vulnerability. His vulnerability was exploited. He opened himself to relationship, and he was ridiculed and killed. If he had arrived as the warrior into the world, this would never have happened. There would have been no vulnerability. But he arrived as a little baby, totally dependent.

So was the life of Jesus a failure because ultimately he died? Does all human life end in failure? We spend our lives trying to prove we are not vulnerable, and yet ultimately it gets us one way or another. Is this failure? Is vulnerability failure?

Two
From Competition to Communion

During the Year of Faith in 2013, I was attending a conference, for all the postprimary teachers in Derry City. At the beginning of the conference I sat beside a friend of mine. On each chair was a small piece of paper with a piece of Scripture on it. I read the piece of Scripture on my chair. I took an instant dislike to it. It was from St. Paul's First Letter to the Corinthians. It read: "You are not your own property, then; you have been bought at a price" (1 Cor. 6:20).

I reacted to this quotation. I showed it to my friend, who agreed that she didn't particularly like it either. There was an empty chair next to her, so she swapped my piece of Scripture for the piece on the empty chair.

I can't remember what that piece of Scripture was, but I was happy with it.

Then, the conference began with a time of prayer. The person leading us in prayer told us that the piece of Scripture we found on our chair was an individual gift from God for each one of us that day. It was in a way God speaking to our heart. Immediately after this was explained, my friend sitting beside me took the piece of Scripture she had given to me away and gave me back the original one. She smiled as she did it!

Why did I react against that original verse? Why did I not want that piece of Scripture? I think that the answer is somewhere around power and control. I want to be in control of my life. I want to have power over my life. I don't want to be answerable to anybody else. I certainly don't want to belong to anyone else. Yet this is exactly what I was being told that morning. I was bought and paid for, and it immediately felt oppressive. This reaction forced me to reflect on power and control.

What does it mean to have power? What does it mean to be in control of my life? For most of us—for me that day!—it is the unquenchable thirst for independence. It is the rejection of vulnerability. It is portrayed as a desire to be upwardly mobile. A successful life is a life that journeys upward and onward, making progress along its way. This way of living creates a pyramid model of society.

Jean Vanier, however, when commenting on Jesus washing the feet of his apostles, says:

> All groups, all societies, are built on the model of the pyramid: at the top are the powerful, the rich, the intelligent. They are called to govern and guide. At the bottom are the immigrants, the slaves, the servants, people who are out of work, or who have a mental illness or different forms of disabilities. They are excluded, marginalized. Here, Jesus is taking the place of a person at the bottom, the last place, the place of a slave. For Peter this is impossible. Little does he realize that Jesus came to transform the model of society from a pyramid to a body, where each and every person has a place, whatever their abilities and

disabilities, where each one is dependent upon the other. Each is called to fulfil a mission in the body of humanity and of the Church. There is no "last place."[1]

The pyramid model is not the model of Jesus. His model was that we would live as his body—that we would live as brothers and sisters, not independent but dependent, acknowledging our mutual vulnerability. We struggle, however, to live that relationship of dependency, of equality and mutual vulnerability, that can ultimately lead to love and acceptance.

We move very quickly from living a relationship of sisters and brothers to living a relationship of fellow competitors. Competition can enter into most of the relationships that we have. That competition can start at a very early age. I don't know if they still have the dreaded bonny baby show! But they used to, and it was awful: putting babies together and picking the best looking. It beggared belief. This still happens, in other forms, in our culture and our lives all the time.

---

1 Jean Vanier, *Drawn into the Mystery of Jesus through the Gospel of John* (London: Darton, Longman and Todd, 2004), 227.

From Competition to Communion

We use competition to motivate people. We use competition to increase people's self-esteem—if they win! Competition can become the way that we most often relate. When a child comes home and tells their parent that they got a B on their test, after the parent says very good, they try to work out how they are going to find out what the rest of the class got so they can see if the B was good or not! Competition drives us so much—too much. It defines so many of our relationships. And in competition, every form of vulnerability must be hidden or beaten.

It is a very small step to go from seeing the other person as a fellow competitor to seeing them as a threat. If that person beats me, I won't get what I want, so they are a threat to me.

The world is trying to make us feel more and more as a threat to one another.

We saw that in a very real way with a recent swine flu epidemic.[2] I am not intending to undermine the need to be careful to curb the spread of a possibly deadly disease, but the swine flu reaction made everybody a threat to everybody else. "Don't touch me because you could contaminate me!" One story about a meeting that happened during the swine flu time has stuck with me. The meeting included people with learning disabilities. Before the beginning of the morning meeting, an announcement was made that due to the swine flu they all had to refrain from hugging that day. Ten minutes after twelve, a boy with Down syndrome went around the room hugging people. When he was asked to stop, he said, "Why? Sure the morning is over!" We can become threats to one another, threats to one another's position, threats to one another's career path, threats to one another's power. We just become threats to one another as we try to climb up the pyramid.

2   The swine flu is a respiratory disease. In 2009, there was a significant outbreak of it that required many precautions to prevent its spread.

It is a very short step to go from seeing the other as a threat to seeing the other as an enemy. Then war breaks out. It is our natural instinct to fight our enemy and show that we are more powerful. It is an understandable journey in many ways to go from being a brother or a sister, to becoming a competitor, to becoming a threat, to becoming an enemy. Maybe all of this happens much easier when we don't live in the context of eternal life. We live just in the context of this world as if our existence here is eternal.

To have power and control is to be at the top of the pyramid. It is to beat others into second place at least. It is to be the best, the most noticed, the most loved, the most admired, the most applauded. It is to be your own woman, your own man, and to have people looking up to you. Somewhere in many of us there seems to be a natural desire for all this to be true. This natural attraction to the top of the pyramid is something that the devil tried to exploit in his encounter with Jesus in the desert (see Matt. 4:1–11). The devil tried to tempt Jesus with the reality of worldly power.

If we give in to the lure of worldly power—the attraction of reaching the top of the pyramid—the first thing we have to do is focus on ourselves. This is what the devil tried to get Jesus to do in the desert. The devil tried to get Jesus to focus only on himself. The devil didn't get into competition with God and say, "I am better." No, instead he made promises to Jesus to make Jesus feel that he was the best, that he was relevant, that he was powerful, that he was spectacular.[3] "I will make you feel good. I will make you feel important. I will make you feel better than all the rest." This was the devil's taunt.

Jesus was in a weak state, so it would have been so easy to give in. Jesus was hungry, so the devil was going to use this place of vulnerability. The devil taunted Jesus to use his power by telling these stones to turn into loaves.

If Jesus had responded to this taunt, he could have cured his own hunger and he could have fed everybody who was hungry. This would have made him feel needed. He would have suddenly been the most relevant of all. The temptation is that it is about me—me being needed, me being relevant. Jesus said no.

3   See Henri Nouwen's book, *In the Name of Jesus: Reflections on Christian Leadership* (New York: Crossroad, 1992), 34.

From Competition to Communion 45

When that didn't work—when Jesus didn't give in to the temptation to be needed, to be relevant—the devil immediately tempted him with the possibility of being spectacular. He brought Jesus to the parapet of the temple and said, "Throw yourself down, for scripture says, 'He will put you in his angels' charge, and they will support you on their hands in case you hurt your foot against a stone.'"

It is the temptation to do the spectacular thing so that you get all the attention. "Look at me. See what I did." Again, the temptation is that it is about me—me being dramatic, me being the center of attention. Jesus said no.

Immediately the devil tempted him again. Jesus rejected the temptations to make himself needed and to make himself spectacular. The devil then tried to tempt him with the possibility of being powerful. He brought Jesus to the top of a very high mountain and showed him all the kingdoms of the earth and their splendor. He said, "I will give you all these." The devil offered Jesus power and glory—to be the boss, to be in charge, to be at the top of the pyramid. Again, the temptation is that it is about me—me being in control, me being number one.

Jesus said no.

Then, the devil gave up.

It takes great courage and confidence not to be lured by the attraction of getting to the top of the pyramid. The devil was very cunning in how he tempted Jesus. What he offered him was extremely attractive. It is attractive to be relevant, to be spectacular, and ultimately to be powerful. What is the cost that we are willing to pay? What is the cost of power? What are we willing to abandon in order to get to the top? Is it power at all costs? Jesus said no. His desire to be relevant wasn't strong enough to overshadow the truth of the necessity of God. He said to the devil: "Man does not live on bread alone but on every word that comes from the mouth of God." The attraction toward being spectacular didn't enable Jesus to abuse the protection of God. He said: "You must not put the Lord your God to the test." The lure of power didn't lead Jesus to the untruth that would undermine God. He said: "You must worship the Lord your God and serve him alone." Jesus stood strong against the intelligence of the devil and faithful to his relationship with his Father, but it is difficult. Power is so attractive.

Worldly power, despite all that we know about its ultimate fragility, is so attractive; and often many compromises can be made and relationships broken just to achieve it. "Get to the top no matter how you do it." We can find evidence of this in the most unexpected places.

John, the Beloved Disciple, made a remarkable journey with Jesus. Depending on which Gospel you read, either he and his brother James asked for seats beside Jesus in his kingdom, or they got their mother to ask on their behalf. We are told in Mark's Gospel that James and John asked Jesus for a favor. They asked: "Allow us to sit one at your right hand and the other at the left in your glory" (Mk. 10:37). In the Gospel according to Matthew, we are told that it was their mother who asked. She said to Jesus: "Promise that these two sons of mine may sit one at your right hand and the other at your left in your kingdom" (Matt. 20:21). It doesn't really matter who asked the question. The sons certainly weren't embarrassed by their mother's request, because when Jesus questioned them further, it was they who answered the questions, not their mother! I have an image of these two boys plotting with their mother about who would be the most effective in asking the question.

In the midst of all that was happening in the public ministry of Jesus, this family was only interested in position. They wanted to be right up at the top of the pyramid. Then they would be seen as the most important. Their mother would be so proud. The boys would have been remarked upon as having done so well. They did better than all the others. This is what matters to most of us too often. Then they would have been relevant and maybe even a bit spectacular. They certainly would have been powerful. They would have been up there beside the most important person. They would have had influence.

They never considered the feelings of their brothers, the other apostles, in their pursuit of the pyramid top. The others were reduced to at least competitors but maybe threats to their desired positions.

More than that, John wanted to use his power. It was not enough for him to be sitting beside the throne. He wanted to show his power by being spectacular. We get evidence of this in the Gospel according to Luke, when Jesus was traveling to Jerusalem (see Lk. 9:51–56). On the way, Jesus went into a Samaritan village where he was not made to feel welcome. James and John had a proposed response to the lack of welcome that they received. They said: "Lord, do you want us to call down fire from heaven to burn them up?"

They were going to show their power. The evidence of their power was going to be spectacular, but it was also going to be destructive. James and John believed they were at the top of the pyramid, and they were going to deal with anybody who didn't respect their position. This is always dangerous. As Pope Francis said in his TED Talk, "Power can be like drinking gin on an empty stomach."[4] Drunk with perceived power, James and John were going to prove that they were the strongest.

Jesus turned and rebuked them. James and John, at this stage, did not understand the reality that Jesus was replacing the pyramid with his body. At this stage, John was obviously attracted to power and position. When Jesus was proclaiming the Good News—when he was telling his closest friends that he would have to suffer and die—John was asking for seats beside him in his kingdom, and threatening violence and destruction to anybody who disagreed with them. He couldn't have been listening to Jesus. He must have been caught up in himself—focusing on himself alone.

This is not the John that we are used to, is it? We think more often about the John as the Beloved Disciple. The one resting on Jesus at the Last Supper, the one standing faithfully at the foot of the cross, the one Jesus entrusted his mother to—this is the John we ordinarily think about. So what happened in John's life to change him? What happened to the John driven by power and position?

4   25th April 2017 –TED.com

The answer must be found when Jesus, at the Last Supper, washed the feet of his disciples. Something must have happened in John at that moment. What Jesus did was outrageous. He got up from the table and knelt down, wrapped a towel around his waist, and started to wash feet. We know how Peter reacted. He was horrified. He objected. He told Jesus that there was no way that he was going to wash his feet. Never! Jesus responded, "If I do not wash you, you can have nothing in common with me" (John 13:8). Then Peter permitted it. However, he still didn't understand. He didn't understand why Jesus did what he did. Peter believed in a powerful Jesus. He believed in a Jesus who was in control, who was the boss. He believed in the pyramid model. The person at the top certainly didn't kneel down and wash feet. When Jesus did what he did, he revealed himself, in the words of Jean Vanier, "as the least one in society, the one who does the dirty jobs, the one who is in the last place."[5]

Jesus chose the place of vulnerability. It took Peter more time to understand and accept this reality about Jesus. Therefore, when Peter denied Jesus three times

5 Vanier, *Drawn into the Mystery of Jesus*, 227.

during the night of Jesus's trial, he wasn't telling lies. The fact is, he didn't yet know this Jesus who washed feet. He didn't recognize the Jesus who didn't fight back and defend himself. The Jesus who was not powerful was a stranger to Peter at that time.

John was different. From his relationship with Jesus after the washing of the feet, it is obvious that John understood what happened. It is only after the washing of the feet that John is described as the "disciple Jesus loved" (John 13:23).

He was reclining next to Jesus. When the difficult question had to be asked—Who was going to betray him?—it was John whom Peter encouraged to ask him. John understood that Jesus's definition of power was not being at the top of the pyramid. It was being at the feet of others, serving them as their brother. John, then, lived this service during the passion and death of Jesus. He is the only apostle named as present at the Crucifixion. John stood at the foot of the cross. John was present to Jesus. He stood with him. He was vulnerable before the crowd. This was not a popular thing to do nor a safe

From Competition to Communion   53

place to be. And then, in this place of vulnerability, John accepted Mary, from Jesus, as his mother. Scriptures tell us, "From that moment the disciple made a place for her in his home" (John 19:27). They were to be dependent on each other.

Jesus didn't send John out on his own, telling him to be strong. He united him with his mother. He created a relationship of care—a relationship built on vulnerability.

John went from a desire for power and position to a place of service and vulnerability. He went from a place of competition to a place of communion. He was no longer looking for the best seats. He no longer needed to be in control. He was united with Jesus and caring for Jesus and his mother. When John started following Jesus, if Jesus had promised at the end of the journey that he could take care of his mother, would John have been satisfied? Yet this is exactly what happened.

John was not powerless. He was, in fact, more powerful than Peter. Peter was afraid. He was confused. John, in the face of all the hatred that existed in the place of the Crucifixion, was present and focused on Jesus.

So what is true power? Is it beating your opponent and proving who is the strongest and most important, or is it serving the other and being present to them? When our definition of power is based on a pyramid model of society, it is a dangerous reality to be engaging in, and it must be something that at best only lasts a short time. Remember Margaret Thatcher! Remember the Beloved Disciple.

Three
From the Need for Power to Discovering Poverty as a Place of Love

It is difficult to make the journey that John made. It is very difficult to see the reality of true and lasting power as opposed to being at the top of the pyramid. It is difficult to live life in the context of eternal life, which is really in the context of a loving and life-giving friendship with Jesus.

We can believe that it feels good to be at the top of the pyramid here and now in this world. In many ways, this is an attractive power. This is the power we have been encouraged to achieve—to be the boss, to own more, to build more, to influence more, to have more. But this power inevitably ends in failure. The greatest people die! The wealthiest people die! The most influential people die! With this type of power the next logical step is not to seek more power, because there can't always be more. The next logical step is to a loss of power. The journey to a loss of power is the journey to poverty. When we leave the top of the pyramid, we must go down. There is no other direction open to us.

There are so many examples of this—the journey from power to poverty. The speed of the journey can differ and the reason for the journey can differ, but the direction of the journey doesn't change. It is always the same. It is a journey that is rarely if ever taken willingly. We always seem to want to hold on to that top spot, so there can be much pain when the direction of the journey changes. There is pain when somebody else puts on our belt and brings us to places we would rather not go. We can see evidence of this in our lives, in the lives of others, and we can see it in public life and in the life of the church.

The financial crash of 2008 was widely reported and commented on. Before the crash, many people were riding on the crest of a wave. Life was never better. There was always more. There was abundance, it seemed, nearly everywhere.

People took financial risks that in the past would not have been imagined. Nothing looked like a risk. There was no end to the money. Houses got bigger and bigger. Independence was what everybody strived for—self-sufficiency. For many, money was no object. In truth, there was obscene wealth and often an obscene use of money that in fact didn't really exist! Then the crash came.

Billions and billions of dollars were simply wiped out. The value of property plummeted. Confidence was destroyed. The power—the uncontrolled power that brought us to the top of the extravagant pyramid—disappeared. What came after the crash was poverty. It was real poverty. People were going bankrupt every day. People were suddenly in negative equity. There was no money. There was no abundance. There was real poverty. It came quickly, and there was no time to prepare for it. Just as the power of the wealth caused many problems, the power of the poverty caused so many more. There was shock and disbelief at what was happening. It wasn't to be this way. The wealth was supposed to be endless. The value of property was supposed to keep increasing. It all went wrong.

Poverty invaded people's lives. There was a financial poverty, but there were also other types of poverty too. There was a poverty of coping skills. People didn't have to learn survival skills during the boom times. During the boom times, we became so much more individualistic. That made the poverty time so much lonelier. The journey from power to poverty is a very painful journey.

A similar example of such a journey from power to poverty is the journey that the Catholic Church has taken in the last few decades in many parts of the world. Sometime between the publication of the Ryan Report and the Murphy Report, which are both government reports that investigated child abuse here in Ireland, a friend of mine spoke to me about being at Mass in his local parish. He remarked that his local priest, who is a good man, was speaking about the importance of protecting children. My friend said that he found it very hard to listen to him. "Why listen to priests talking about safeguarding children?" my friend said. I was shocked. My friend is a reasonable person, who attends Mass, yet he had this very strong reaction to his priest speaking about child protection—speaking about what should be a fundamental part of preaching the Gospel. At first I was offended by my friend's attitude. Could people be reacting to me speaking in a similar way?

I never believed that I would be associated with those who abused children. It was a poverty I never thought I would have to face. This was probably naivete on my part. I naively thought I could always distance myself from those in the ordained ministry who abused children. But it is not so simple. It is not so simple because not only did brother priests abuse children, but also brother priests who were bishops covered up this abuse. It is also not so simple because the abuse crisis and the way it was handled seem to be a manifestation of a deep structural problem. That deep structural problem seems to be rooted in an abuse of power.

On Vocation Sunday a number of years ago, I heard a priest who was ordained in 1956 say in his homily that, upon reflection, he now felt that as seminarians they were treated as battery hens! Individuality was consistently frowned upon. Conformity to rules and regulations was all that seemed important. Then as now, there seems to be an obsession with power and control. People at the top of the pyramid often seen to control those below them.

This desire for control and use and abuse of power have led the Church to a place of great poverty in many parts of the world. This poverty is a place of great confusion and insecurity where much that we created to give us our identity seems to be eroded. It seems to be very clear that many of those who dealt with the issue of the abuse of children by priests were driven by an abuse of power and a need to control. They did not want anything to happen that would undermine what they had, so they used their power sadly to hide the truth. Hiding the truth denied the Gospel. It also left some in the Church as prisoners of their past deeds.

The Church should be the last place where power is abused because the Church is called to be the presence of Jesus in the world. The Church's sole purpose is to proclaim the Good News of Jesus Christ. This Good News is a message of compassion and mercy. So what happened? How does the likes of the Church abuse power and become obsessed with power? Henri Nouwen, when speaking about Christian leadership, says:

> The temptation to consider power an apt instrument for the proclamation of the Gospel is the greatest of all. We keep hearing others, as well as saying ourselves, that having power—provided it is used in the service of God and your fellow human beings—is a good thing. With this rationalization, crusades took place; inquisitions were organized; Indians were enslaved; positions of great influence were desired; episcopal palaces, splendid cathedrals, and opulent seminaries were built; and much moral manipulation of conscience was engaged in. Every time we see a major crisis in the history of the Church . . . we

always see that a major cause of rupture is the power exercised by those who claim to be followers of the poor and powerless Jesus.[6]

The reality that our Savior chose to be poor and powerless, to be vulnerable, is probably the greatest obstacle to faith. Jesus positively chose poverty that came from vulnerability instead of power. It would seem to be so much easier to believe in Jesus and follow his example if he had worldly power, position, and influence. This is what Peter looked for for so long, as did James and John. The fact that Jesus lived outside of the power structure of society, outside the accepted pyramid, was too hard to accept. He did not force anybody to follow him, and that's a model of leadership we struggle to understand. Jesus controlled nobody. He wielded power over nobody except the devil (see Lk. 4:31–37). He was free, and he allowed others to be free too. His harshest words were for those who tried to control others—those who were hypocritical—those who wanted to be

---

6   Henri J. M. Nouwen, *In the Name of Jesus: Reflections on Christian Leadership* (New York: Crossroad, 1992), 58.

recognized and greeted in the market place—those who wore fine robes—those who placed intolerable burdens on others (see Matt. 23:4–7).

Sadly, many people in leadership seem to be easily seduced by worldly power to get to the top of the pyramid. Poverty is avoided. We have built earthly empires and have tried to create structures to maintain these empires. The empires and the structures give us much of our identity.

Our commitment to worldly power reveals a crisis of faith and a lack of trust in our poor, powerless Savior to save us. It is the attitude of Peter at the washing of the feet (see John 13:1–17). We have demonstrated that we are unable to trust in Jesus—in the one who has called us and the one who trusts us.

Before we become too critical of others, many of us have the same attitude. Many of us thought that money would save us. The more we had, the more powerful we were. We thought position saves us. We thought having influence saves us. Often we think we can save ourselves—we are like gods in our own finite world. Then we have no need of God, or anybody else for that matter, in these circumstances.

Maybe the God who entered the world as the defenseless baby of Bethlehem doesn't really suit us. The Messiah who let the rich young man go might seem too poor for us (see Mk. 10:17–31). The one who was rejected, defeated, and crucified, who needed his mother as he died on the cross, is probably too vulnerable for us. Yet this is the one who has confidence in us to be his presence in the world today. This is the one who believes that we are weak enough and vulnerable enough to be his love and compassion. Jesus reveals this when he says to his disciples after his resurrection: "Go out to the whole world; proclaim the Good News" (Mk. 16:15). It is an incredible trust in a remarkable time in history.

So how do we break out of the structure that facilitates an abuse of power? I'm not sure. It is painful but ultimately liberating. How do we stop allowing ourselves to be seduced by the top of the pyramid? How do we see the truth of worldly power? How do we live our lives in the context of eternal life and so accept the incompleteness of this life? How do we live as sisters and brothers?

Simply, we need to follow the example of Jesus. Jesus introduced a way for living into this world that is superior to all other ways. His way is radical and upsets many accepted ways of living. However, the way of Jesus lasts and bears fruit if it is faithfully lived because it is not focused on the self but always on the good of others.

The story of the good Samaritan really captures the way of Jesus (see Lk. 10:25–37). Perhaps to embrace this way of Jesus we need to see trust and vulnerability as gifts from God. Ironically, these gifts are more powerful than any earthly power. They are the gift of humble service. By embracing this gift of humble service and admitting the reality of our poverty, we reject the abuse of power. We share in the life of Jesus, who "emptied himself, taking the form of a slave" (Phil. 2:7).

Our poor, powerless Savior chose to use the power of God to serve others, to empower others, to enable others to believe in themselves and trust themselves. The power of service enables us to "rise up with all the gifts we have and then kneel down to help others, so that we can have a world where there is more peace."[7]

Maybe this gift of service that God is giving us could be described as the sacrament of poverty. To accept this gift, maybe we need to surrender. Maybe we need to surrender the empire, the safe existence, the position in the pyramid, our created identity. Maybe we need to trust in the poor, powerless Savior whose only power is the power to save us. Maybe we need to live in the body of Christ where everybody is necessary, valued, and accepted.

Maybe this is not impossible to do. It is happening in a small way already.

The L'Arche community was founded by Jean Vanier in 1964. Jean began the community by welcoming two men from a mental asylum into his home. Today there are 147 L'Arche communities in thirty-five countries in the world. The aims of the L'Arche community perhaps

---

7   Jean Vanier, lecture, "Choosing Your Future Conference," Millennium Forum, Derry, Northern Ireland, 2009.

reveal what the aims of any nation, community, church, family, and indeed personal life could and should be. Their aims include giving a valid place in society for the rejected as well as revealing the gifts of the weak and the vulnerable and listening to their call. L'Arche does not aim to give answers to society but to be a sign to society that to be human means welcoming and respecting the weak and the downtrodden. L'Arche always aims to be a sign of hope founded on a covenant relationship between people who are different.

Imagine putting the weak and the vulnerable at the heart of all that we do. They would call us out of ourselves into a new, radical way of living and loving. That these aims can be embraced and lived is clear to be seen in many of the L'Arche communities throughout the world. The L'Arche community lives the sacrament of poverty.

Maybe L'Arche, living the sacrament of poverty, shows us how to live the way of Jesus in these times. The sacrament of poverty would enable us to realize that we are not God and that we always need God. It would liberate us from the need to protect or to save ourselves.

Sr. Maria Boulding, a Benedictine sister from England, reflecting on her life as she became increasingly weak through cancer, said:

> I have discovered that suffering and happiness are by no means incompatible; on the contrary, my weakness seems to help. New understanding of friendship, love and tenderness has been given. There is a way to walk, even as I grow weaker. Love is communicated at levels of shared suffering, tenderness and bodily care that I have never touched before, and my weakness has been needed to open them. . . . I am able now to accept the love of others, and believe in it, like a helpless child who has nothing to give except its need. Now, when I am useless, can do little in the way of work and cannot make a difference, all I can give is my need of other people. . . . Letting go and letting God, loss of independence and self-sufficiency, being freed from the need to be useful and to justify one's existence by any kind of achievement—these may be liberation and a way into deeper love.[8]

---

8 Maria Boulding, "New Bend in the Road—a Reflection at the End of Life," *The Tablet* (London, UK), April 3, 2010.

Sr. Maria was not fighting against her suffering—her poverty. She was living it aware that in and through it she was being led on a sacred journey with and to God. Perhaps our gift to each other and to the world today is the gift of our need. Maybe that is the most profound gift that any of us can give to another. The gift of our poverty enables us to be open to loving, life-giving relationships.

Jean Vanier is aware of the poverty of the L'Arche community. When speaking about the future of L'Arche, he often says that L'Arche is fragile and may not exist tomorrow. He does not say this with any fear or anxiety. There is a great freedom and a trust in his ability to embrace the fragility of L'Arche. I think we fear to admit the fragility of our lives. Yet even the risen body of Jesus was fragile because Jesus was still wounded (see John 20:20). It was by his wounds that he was recognized.

Yes, Jesus founded the Church on the rock of Peter— on his relationship with Peter. But even the strongest rock can be blasted and broken. All of this can be too difficult to face. For Jean Vanier in L'Arche, and Sr. Maria Boulding as she faced her death, the fact and the beauty of poverty is clear. However, this is not the case for everybody.

It is a real struggle and often seemingly impossible to see poverty in a positive way. The poverty that the Church experiences today for many is a loss and a shame. The poverty that people who have gone bankrupt face is a loss and a shame. Going from the top of the pyramid to the bottom is a loss and a shame. For many of the followers of Jesus, his crucifixion and death were a loss and a shame. Hope died on the cross. People must have regretted following Jesus. He was supposed to be the winner, but he lost. We have evidence of this lost hope in the two people on the road to Emmaus (see Lk. 24:13–35). We're told that their faces were downcast. They began their story by saying, "Our own hope had been." Hope was in the past tense.

So, for many people, the journey from power to poverty is a journey of lost hope and broken dreams and not a road ever to be chosen.

Four
From Humiliation to Acceptance of Who We Really Are

I don't believe that our lives follow a straight line. Our life line is at least crooked, and for many it is perhaps more like a spiral than anything else. However, I do believe that certain situations inevitably lead to certain conclusions.

If worldly success in life is measured by being at the top of the pyramid, or if it is considered being independent of need of others, then in at least one important respect, all human life ends in failure, as the world defines failure.

The loss of power, and indeed control, leaves us feeling poor, vulnerable, and weak. These are feelings that many of us try to avoid because the world defines them as failure. They are feelings that often fill us with dread and fear. This is common to all people everywhere. We often see how desperately governments try to cling to power, and how some people with money or power (including, sadly, leaders in our churches) will desperately cling to it, whatever it takes. We want to stay in control because we do not want to appear poor, vulnerable, or weak. To give in to this poverty is to give in to incompleteness. We don't want our lives to be incomplete. However—in this world—incompleteness seems to be inevitable. We need to accept that, understand it, and even embrace our incompleteness as our calling, if we want to follow the path of Jesus.

It is inevitable that we cannot have power forever, and the journey from power is the journey toward poverty. As Christians, we are called to be poor. The beatitude tells us: "Blessed are the poor in spirit" (Matt. 5:3). In the Gospel, we are called to material poverty. We are told very clearly that Jesus lives in those who are poor, and whatever we do to the least, we do to Jesus himself (see Matt. 25:40). If we want to see Jesus in the world, we will see him most clearly in those who are poor. This is not simply metaphor. "Poor" means, at least in part, those who are without an adequate share of things that sustain human life.

Jesus was himself poor, and he felt most at home with the poor. He was not a member of the rich or ruling classes. Sometimes we can glamorize Jesus's relationship with the poor. We can marvel at the choice he made to be so associated with poor people, almost as if he wasn't with those who have little or nothing. I think that is to miss the point. Jesus was a poor man himself, and therefore with the poor was the natural place for him to be. It is there that he obviously felt at home.

It is easy to glamorize the poor. Sometimes we make poverty into a metaphor as we pray for a "spirit of poverty." We marvel at how close to God many of those who are poor seem to be. We marvel at their simplicity and maybe even their joy. But it's easy to neglect the simple fact of the circumstances of those who are without.

People with disabilities are some of the poorest people on the planet. In a world that promotes and demands ability and mobility, they are left behind. So are the homeless, refugees, and, increasingly, immigrants. There is nothing attractive about being poor. Ask somebody who is living on the street how it feels. The poor are those whom society has left behind because they do not fit in. It is painful when you don't fit in. Those who are poor are at the bottom of the pyramid of society. It is painful when we depend on the charity of another for our basic needs. It is painful not to be loved and appreciated. At the end of the day, we simply don't want to be poor. There is nothing glamorous about it.

Whether we like it or not, the institutional church today has gone from a place of worldly power and control to a place of poverty. For the most part, we react very badly to our newfound poor status. We are desperately trying to cling to our power. Yes, we pray to be poor and humble, but not like this. We don't want to be really poor, without position or reputation. Maybe we want to be poor in a controlled and glamorized way.

If we continue the straight-line approach to life, power inevitably leads to poverty, but poverty inevitably leads to humiliation. With poverty, there comes humiliation. Being humiliated is different than being humble. To be humble in a sense is our own choice. To be humiliated is to experience the negative reaction of others to us. Nobody wants to be humiliated. It is horrible.

Christians are called to be the body of Christ. Christians are called to live as Christ—to share in his life. This removes the pyramid model of society with its competition, threats, and enemies—and we see this in the heart of the Eucharist. We receive the body of Christ, and we are called to be the body of Christ. It was Pope St. Leo the Great who said: "Our participation in the body and blood of Christ has the effect of making us become what we receive. The body and blood enable us, with our whole being, in our spirit and our flesh, to bear him in whom and with whom we have died and been buried and risen again."[9] We often pray to be humble enough to do this—to share fully in the life of Jesus. We

---

9   Pope St. Leo the Great, Sermon 12 on the Passion, 3:7. Various translations.

pray that we will serve those who are poor as Jesus did. We might even go so far as to pray that we will be poor or at least realize our own poverty. But how many of us pray to be humiliated? You may object and say, "But this is not necessary. This is going too far."

However, if we are serious about sharing fully in the life of Jesus, then humiliation is an inevitable part. Jesus was humiliated. He was humiliated when he was tied to a pillar and flogged in public view. He was humiliated when he was crowned with a crown of thorns and dressed in a purple robe. He was humiliated when he was stripped of his garments, and his broken, bruised, and bloodied body was revealed for all to see. He was humiliated when he was nailed to a cross and died a defeated man in the eyes of many. The one in whose life we are called to share was humiliated. This is a part of Jesus's life that we don't want to enter. We want to wear protective clothing before being flogged. Maybe we accept the crown of thorns, but we want to dress it up in diamonds first. We know that we need to be stripped of our garments, but we want to have our clothes on when the stripping is over. Yes, we know that crucifixion is part of the story, but we try to glamorize and sanitize it as best we can. We fight against humiliation, and understandably so, but ultimately we will lose the fight. Humiliation is part of the story, and it comes from poverty.

In the straight-line approach to life, we have gone from power to poverty, from poverty to humiliation. Where do we go when we are humiliated? Here is where the line goes in at least two directions—maybe three—and we have a choice. Maybe this is the only power we have in humiliation. It is the power to decide. We can react or respond in two major ways to humiliation and perhaps in a third. We can choose freedom or paralysis. A natural reaction to humiliation is to be paralyzed by it. This paralysis manifests itself in two very clear ways—in anger and shame.

When we are humiliated, we can become angry. We can become arrogant and defensive. We can fight. We can see some of these characteristics in one of the men crucified with Jesus. See Luke 23:39. He goaded Jesus. He told him to save himself and the thieves as well. This man was paralyzed with anger. He could not see beyond it. His humiliation had made him a prisoner, and all he could do was lash out at others from the prison of his cross.

Humiliation can also lead to deep shame. It can cause people to want to curl up, hide, and die. The shame that humiliation can bring can be immense, and again this can cause deep paralysis. This can lead to death. We have evidence of this in a dramatic way in Judas, the disciple of Jesus who betrayed him after the events of the Last Supper and the Garden of Gethsemane. Judas pointed Jesus out to the Romans, and we are told that after Jesus was taken prisoner, Judas became filled with remorse—filled with shame. He told the priests and the elders, "'I have sinned. I have betrayed innocent blood.' They replied, 'What is that to us? That is your concern.' And flinging down the silver pieces in the sanctuary he made off, and went and hanged himself" (Matt. 27:3–5).

Whether our reaction to humiliation is anger or shame, the result is a deep isolationism and death. The angry person becomes isolated because they become so defensive and arrogant that they are unable to communicate with others. They are unable to form relationships. The person full of shame is isolated, too, because they cut themselves off and just want to hide. They are also unable to form relationships because they don't think that anybody could possibly love them in their poverty.

But there is another reaction to humiliation—it is freedom. This sounds like an impossible choice, but hear me out. If the power of humiliation is paralysis and death, how can that power be broken? How, when we are at our lowest point, can we find the energy to break the power of what brought us to that point? The answer is this: freedom comes when we accept reality, but when we don't allow that reality to control us.

Jesus is the greatest example of freedom that we have. He accepted the reality of his crucifixion, but he saw beyond it. He didn't allow his crucifixion and all that went with it to control him. He refused to give in to the temptation to focus on himself or the pain that he was suffering. He chose freedom, and in his freedom, he gave his mother to John and John to his mother. He continued to care for others. I believe that his example inspired the other man crucified with him to choose freedom too. This man witnessed Jesus on the cross. He witnessed the encounter that he had with those at the foot of the cross. He was so inspired by what he witnessed that he could see the truth of his own situation and was free to encounter Jesus. He did not allow anger or shame to stop him. In his encounter with Jesus, this man experienced life. He didn't say to Jesus, "Let's die here together as friends." No, he saw beyond his present situation and humbly asked Jesus to remember him in his kingdom. This man was not living his life in context of this world only. He was living his life in the context of eternal life. The response he received from Jesus was eternal life. Jesus said to him: "Today you will be with me in paradise" (Lk. 23:43).

When we choose freedom as our response to humiliation, that same humiliation and poverty will lead to encounter, and the encounter gives life—eternal life. We see this in Jesus's own choice and also in the man crucified with him. Neither allowed their humiliation to control them, and neither denied their humiliation.

I mentioned the possibility of there being a third response to humiliation, apart from freedom or paralysis. This third direction is self-doubt. It is this direction that leads you to a place where you don't have the energy or the confidence to choose either freedom or the paralysis that comes from anger or shame.

When humiliation destroys our confidence, we can neither say to Jesus, "If you are that great, save me and yourself too," nor can we say, with the man crucified beside Jesus, "Remember me when you come into your kingdom." This place of profound self-doubt takes all the energy from us. It is the place of defeat. It is a place where compulsions can develop and control us.

These compulsions often manifest themselves in alcohol or drug abuse, in sexual abuse of self and others, in pornography, in so many ways that we can express our total lack of confidence. This is a different paralysis that blinds us to life. It can lead to deep negativity—"Nothing will work; nothing will ever be right again." In this place of self-doubt, the only comfort we will get is in remembering the time before humiliation and wishing for that time to be created again. We lose our identity. We lose our energy, and we keep looking at the past to find the future that cannot be found.

I suppose the question that needs to be asked is whether self-doubt is a choice or not. In some ways, we might be able to choose anger or freedom, but are we not inflicted with self-doubt? We don't choose to doubt ourselves. We don't positively surrender our confidence. Circumstances erode our confidence. Maybe it is more accurate to say that we can allow circumstances to erode our confidence. The apostles give us a wonderful example of this when they are out in the boat with Jesus. Take a look at the Gospel of Mark 4:35–41.

Jesus is asleep, and the storm grows and Jesus remains asleep. The apostles start to panic, and eventually they wake Jesus, essentially asking him, "Don't you care?" Basically, he responds to them by saying, "You seem to have no faith in yourselves." His words were these: "Why are you so frightened? How is it that you have no faith?" Jesus believed in the apostles. He believed in their ability to steer the boat home in very rough seas. The problem was that the apostles didn't have enough confidence in themselves. Their self-doubt had taken control.

When we lose sight of the source of our confidence, we give in to self-doubt. This is obviously what happened when Peter jumped out of the boat at another time when he saw Jesus walking on the water (see Matt. 14:22–33). While Peter was focused on Jesus, he too was able to walk on water. But as soon as Peter stopped looking at Jesus and allowed himself to focus on the wind and the water under his feet, he started to sink. Then he had to call out and reach out to Jesus to save him. Jesus, the source of his confidence, the one who believes in him, is the one who saves Peter when he loses focus.

Humiliation makes it difficult to focus on reality. Self-doubt tries to remove us from reality. Anger and bitterness lead us in many ways to try to resent reality. Only freedom allows us to face reality and not be controlled by it.

Five
Fruits from Humiliation

So humiliation can lead us in one of three directions. It can lead us toward freedom, or to the paralysis of anger and shame, or to the different paralysis of self-doubt. Which would you prefer in your life?

To go in the direction of freedom, how should we deal with our humiliation? And is it possible to choose one of these paths for ourselves, or is it inevitable that most of us will give in to either the paralysis of self-doubt or the paralysis of anger and shame?

In this present time of humiliation for the institutional church, there is a real danger that those who love our church will choose the road of paralysis that comes from anger or shame. For some of us, this can be the road of anger and defensiveness. We can use all our energy to defend our worldly power that has long since gone. We can become arrogant and deny our humiliation and declare that it is everybody else who is wrong. We can become angry and retaliate toward those we believe we can still control. For others of us, we can be full of shame. We may just want to hide—maybe try to walk away. We can try to privatize our faith and our practice. We can surround ourselves with like-minded people and try to ease the pain of the shame or the anger. All of this inevitably paralyzes us and will ultimately lead to death. The shame and the anger will just eat us up and sap our energy and take our lives. These are understandable reactions to humiliation, but they are also destined never to bring with them life.

Instead, we need to keep considering the other way forward, individually, and as a people of God. There are other ways of dealing with our humiliation.

I want to introduce you to a man named Jeffrey. Jeffrey is an ordinary human being, if such a person exists. But

Jeffrey had every reason to be angry. Particularly, he had every reason to be angry with his father. Jeffrey's father suffered from an alcohol addiction that destroyed him and affected his relationship with his wife and his children. He was a very difficult man and made home a painful place. He was a bully and often nasty. Jeffrey witnessed this throughout his young life. One result was that he became very protective of his mother. She was a wonderful person who was so full of life and energy and love. In many ways, she was a complete contradiction to her husband. At one point in his teenage years, Jeffrey even hit his father in defense of his mother.

Jeffrey had every right to hate his father. His father did nothing to deserve his love. It would have been completely understandable if Jeffrey put his father out of his life. After Jeffrey's mother died, he could have left his father to sink or swim on his own. However, Jeffrey chose to be faithful to his dad. This was difficult to do because his father never stopped drinking. He always had the potential to be nasty.

I used to observe so clearly that Jeffrey was not a dutiful son. What he did he didn't do simply out of duty. There was more. For a long time, I couldn't understand what the more was. I don't think it was affection, but it was more than duty. Whatever it was, it was the key to choosing freedom in the face of humiliation. What was this key that opened the door to Jeffrey's freedom? It is the key that allowed Jesus to say to the thief: "Today you will be with me in paradise."

One day, Jeffrey's father became ill. It was a serious sickness that meant he had to be admitted to a hospital. Then came the bad news that Jeffrey's father had a form of rapidly spreading terminal cancer. He was dying. I witnessed Jeffrey accompanying his father to the moment of death. I witnessed pure, unconditional love. The tenderness with which Jeffrey treated his father revealed the highest level of human maturity.

For example, because Jeffrey knew that massaging his father's feet gave his dad great comfort, he gently and lovingly did that as often as he could. There was no awkwardness, just love. That love came from a place of great freedom because it came from a place of absolute reality. There were no rose-tinted glasses worn for the past. There was no airbrushing. Neither was there any anger or arrogance. It was just pure love. It was a time of mutual vulnerability.

It also became a love that Jeffrey's father recognized and acknowledged that he didn't deserve. But the freedom that Jeffrey had enabled him to love anyway. It was one of the most profound examples of somebody choosing freedom in the face of humiliation that I have ever witnessed. Even after Jeffrey's dad's death, the freedom that was a fruit of love continued as Jeffrey has continued to get to know his father better and better and understand more and more the humiliation his father felt that led him to those places of terrible self-doubt and anger and destruction. Jeffrey still shows that the compassion and freedom of Jesus on the cross is possible today too.

The freedom of Jesus is not just possible today; it is absolutely necessary. It is necessary because there is so much humiliation in the world. People are being humiliated all the time. One example of this came after the economic crash of 2008. The time before the crash was an unreal time when wealth and the accumulation of wealth was the driving force for so many (especially in Ireland, where we became so pleased with ourselves and our "Celtic Tiger" economy). People were trying to buy their way to the top of the pyramid. With the accumulation of this unreal wealth, because it didn't actually exist, a lavish lifestyle emerged. Then came the crash, and with the poverty the crash brought there came so much humiliation. The unreality that wealth brought security was laid bear when people were declared bankrupt. People went from living like millionaires to not having enough money to pay for their basic needs. It was devastating. It continues to be so for many people. How do you cope with this humiliation—the humiliation of the change from being the wealthy one to being the poor one? How do you cope with the humiliation of

Fruits from Humiliation

publicly being declared bankrupt? How do you cope with the humiliation of losing your home? How do you cope with the humiliation of your family breaking apart because life has changed so much? How do you cope?

In many ways, the natural reaction to this might be the third choice. It is the choice that leads to self-doubt. It is the choice that leads to an erosion of confidence. It can lead to compulsions, or to total paralysis and death. It is the choice that can lead to a completely defeatist negative attitude that allows you to believe the best days are behind you and the only forward is to re-create the past.

There is another way, and it's no good for us either. There is the way of anger. It can be the time to blame everybody and everything else. It is all the politicians' fault. It is the fault of the banks. It is everybody's fault but mine. The anger brings paralysis too. Then there is the shame. People are so ashamed that their life has been such a public failure. It is the shame of having to live in a different house, drive a different car, shop in different shops. The shame is paralyzing too. How in the face of this public humiliation is it possible to choose freedom?

To choose freedom, it is vital to acknowledge the incompleteness of our lives. In an economic boom, the tendency is to build up treasure here on earth.

During the economic crash, I met a man named Pio. Pio was a successful businessperson. The world was his oyster, and money was no object. But he suffered terribly in the crash. He was declared bankrupt. Life changed dramatically. However, what was remarkable about Pio were the choices that he made in the midst of his humiliation. The first choice he made was the most liberating of all: to live in reality. Pio was able to look back and see the truth of his past. He was able to honestly assess what had motivated him. He was able to see clearly in the present and name what mattered most of all to him. His relationship with money began to change, and as his relationship with money changed, so did his relationship with God, with Jesus, with others, and with work.

Pio will, still today, say that he had no choice in what he did after his business collapsed. But we always have choices. Pio was like the apostles after the Crucifixion. In many ways, for them, the dream was dead. The result of years of energy and work seemed to have come to nothing. It too was a kind of bankruptcy. After the Crucifixion, the apostles locked themselves away in fear and, no doubt, shame. Then we know what happened. Jesus came among them (see John 20:19–23). Jesus gave them two gifts. The first gift was the gift of peace: "Peace be with you." Then he did something remarkable and strange.

The obvious thing would have been for Jesus to tell the apostles to go out and tell everybody that he, Jesus, was alive and that the apostles had been right all along. However, he didn't do this. Jesus sent the apostles out with the power to forgive sins. In other words, Jesus sent them out with the power to free people from their past.

In the face of humiliation, Pio chose not to go down the road of fear and shame. He chose not to lock himself away in self-doubt. It is particularly difficult not to allow shame to control you when your humiliation is public and ongoing. Rather than a time of paralysis, Pio saw this as the time of necessary growth and new life. He was being pruned, and it was painful. But proper pruning enables stronger growth, even as it makes the plant vulnerable.

Pio accepted the gift of peace and allowed himself to be released from his past through the gift of forgiveness. In doing this, by facing reality, Pio's vulnerability allowed his confidence to grow. When we deny our vulnerability, we become arrogant. When we are arrogant, we stunt our growth. Arrogance prohibits growth—in fact, arrogance is like cement poured over a seed.

As Pio's confidence began to grow, it did not grow according to his own work and efforts alone. His confidence grew as his relationship with Jesus grew. This makes perfect sense because Jesus is the root of our confidence. Remember him sleeping in the boat? Jesus believes in us to collaborate with him. When we focus on Jesus, we can, like Peter, walk on water. When our friendship with Jesus deepens, we realize more and more that we have been called and chosen. We have a specific trust placed in us by God. In the words of St. John Henry Newman: "God has created me to do Him some definite service. He has committed some work to me which He has not committed to another. I have my mission."[10]

---

10 This is from a prayer-poem first published just after Newman's death. See St. John Henry Newman, *Meditations and Devotions* (Brewster, MA: Paraclete Press, 2019).

Pio grew in his awareness and trust that God was enabling him to begin again. This new beginning was not an attempt to re-create the past. It had a clearer vision and mission—a bigger vision and mission. Yes, money has to be made for survival and life, but our primary call is to collaborate with God in his ongoing creation and his ongoing dream for our lives.

In his humiliation, Pio wrote a prayer for himself and for other men he knew in the same situation. He called it a "Prayer for Business." He doesn't mind my sharing it with you. Pio prayed:

Lord, show us the way.
Fill our minds with ideas that are good for us and for all humanity.
Fill us with the Holy Spirit; make us your instruments.
Make us good family men.
Guide us to be a positive influence on all we meet on the journey.
Help us to see everything through your eyes.
Give us confidence to go forward, knowing that we are your sons.
Above all your will be done. Amen.

The rootedness to God, obvious in this prayer, gave Pio tremendous courage. The evidence of his courage was that he started again, and also that he started with different motivation and methods. He knew that the old methods belonged to the old way. New wine cannot go into old wineskins, as Jesus taught in one of his parables (see Matt. 9:14–17). Now, Pio was living life in a larger context. It was not life in that old, ungodly pyramid. It was life in the body of Christ, the body that has defeated death. This time, for instance, he knew that he wanted to teach his children the dignity of work, their dignity as members of the body of Christ, not just competitors in a pyramid.

Pio chose freedom, rather than paralysis and death, in the face of his humiliation. That freedom is a vulnerable place, but it is a better one. It is the place of reality and truth. And Pio is very clear that this is the best place from which to bear positive witness to others in the generations to come.

Six
All Things Pass Away

St. Teresa of Avila's bookmark—found after the saint's death, inscribed by her on a prayer card, stuck in her breviary—tells us:

> Let nothing disturb you, nothing affright you.
> All things pass away.
> God alone remains.
> Patience obtains all it asks for.
> God alone suffices.

She knew: All things pass away. God alone suffices.

We are living through a time when all things are passing away. We are recovering from the last economic crisis; but fresh, not unfounded, fears are that the recovery is based on basically re-creating the system that caused the last crisis. It seems inevitable that the financial structures of the past are in their dying days. If so, another crash (there will always be crashes) will result in more humiliation for more people.

We cannot continue, in many respects, the way we have been going. Fifty years ago, if you told people that they were able to buy things without having the money to do so, they would have laughed; it would have sounded absurd. But, of course, we do it all the time today. It is absurd. It cannot last. There will be terrible pain when this system comes to an end. But all things pass away.

When an economic system passes away, it is difficult to have peace. It seems that our world sees less peace between people than ever before. We seem, in fact, to have accepted that a certain measure of strife and war is somehow normal. Pope Francis has said that the world is at war. He is right. We are living through the world at war. Not long ago, the political and social philosopher Eric Hobsbawm wrote, "The world as a whole has not been at peace since 1914, and is not at peace now."¹¹ He too is right. We see it all around us. We live with it. Well, it isn't "normal."

We live surrounded by opportunities in our lives for more humiliation, suffering, and death. We are coming to the end of the post–Second World War era. It has been a time that brought people together and broke down walls. The European Union was created; the fall of Communism, with the physical collapse of the Berlin Wall, took place. But now we are back to building walls again. We are retreating behind walls and closed doors, and we are acting out of fear.

We also seem to be coming to the end of the era of liberalism and excessive focus on the individual. We have lived through decades of an increasing belief that anything goes; but this ends in respect for nothing—not even ourselves. We seem to be coming to the end of the era of rights without responsibilities and actions without consequences. We've come to see that in a liberal agenda that places excessive focus on the individual, the ultimate destination must be a dead end. How do we live in this time? How do we face what is to come?

11 War and Peace in the 20th Century 21st February 2002 –https://www.lrb.co.uk/v24/n04/eric-hobsbawm/war-and-peace-in-the-20th-century

I suggest we look to the Catholic Church in Algeria to help us answer these questions. Let me explain.

The Church in Algeria choose freedom in a dramatic way when they faced the humiliation of persecution and death. They'd lost everything. Once, they were a powerful institution in the country. They ran schools and hospitals. Then, facing unfriendly political powers, they aggressively lost all these institutions; indeed, all foreigners in the country were asked to leave. Since the Church was mostly a missionary Church, this request to leave had a direct effect. By staying, they would be risking their lives. Missionaries remaining in Algeria would have to suffer the humiliation of losing their jobs in the schools and hospitals and trying to find new jobs in state-run schools and hospitals. Even if they got a job, they would be living in fear for their lives.

The natural choice they could have made was to leave the country. They also could have become angry or defensive. They could have become ashamed at their loss of power and position. They could have lost their confidence. They could have left Algeria and condemned it and justified their leaving. But they chose to stay. In the face of humiliation, they freely stayed in a very dangerous environment.

The reason they stayed is summed up in what they came to call the "Sacrament of Encounter." This Sacrament of Encounter emerged as a direct fruit of the Church in Algeria choosing freedom as their response to humiliation. They chose to stay and enable others to encounter Jesus by encountering them. That's the Sacrament of Encounter. Ask an Algerian Catholic leader, and they will tell you: "We are not aiming to convert Muslims. We do not want to fight with anyone. We are not defensive over what has happened to us, in our country, and we do not intend to hide. We simply want Jesus to be present to the people of Algeria through us."

Martin McGee, OSB, in his book *Christian Martyrs for a Muslim People*, explains the demands of the Sacrament of Encounter:

This new approach or emphasis on encounter, what the Church in Algeria calls the sacrament of encounter, is much more demanding of the missionary, as the quality of his own life becomes the key to the proclamation of the Gospel. In the past, the sacraments worked regardless of the person administrating them. Now the sacrament of encounter depends on the person's closeness to God, on him being a clear medium through which the love of God is passed on to another person, and on his receptivity to accepting God's love from another person. This requires much more from the missionaries than simply answering the questions or putting up new buildings, however necessary these answers or buildings may be. The effectiveness of this sacrament depends on the transparency of Christ's presence and love in the individual Christian and in his or her community.[12]

The Church in Algeria chose to be the presence of Jesus. It is only possible to be the presence of Jesus if you have the faith to recognize Jesus—God—alive in all those

---

12 Martin McGee, OSB, *Christian Martyrs for a Muslim People* (Mahwah, NJ: Paulist Press, 2008), 67.

you meet. This reflects St. Teresa's breviary bookmark prayer: God alone remains. Br. Henri, a Trappist monk who was martyred in Algeria, said when speaking about the other—the one who is different—who is perhaps the one we struggle to love and accept: "It is not enough to tolerate the other. We are called to identify the unique gift that God has given the other and marvel at it."[13] This is such a dramatic expression of freedom in the face of humiliation.

One of the greatest expressions of the freedom that is possible in the face of humiliation, however, comes from the prior of the Abbey of Our Lady of Atlas in Tibhirine, Christian de Chergé. He was also a Trappist monk in Algeria, martyred along with sixteen others for their faith. The film *Of Gods and Men* tells their story. Christian was a man of the deepest freedom. Evidence of this is found in his last testament, which he wrote to be opened and read if he died by violence. The text was opened on the feast of Pentecost in 1996, shortly after the monks were killed. In it, he writes:

13 Ibid Page 34

If it should happen one day—and it could be today—that I become a victim of the terrorism which now seems ready to encompass all the foreigners living in Algeria, I would like my community, my Church, my family, to remember that my life was given to God and to this country. I ask them to accept that the One Master of all life was not a stranger to this brutal departure. . . .

I could not desire such a death. It seems to me important to state this. I do not see, in fact, how I could rejoice if this people I love were to be accused indiscriminately of my murder. It would be to pay too dearly for what will, perhaps, be called "the grace of martyrdom," to owe it to an Algerian, whoever he may be, especially if he says he is acting in fidelity to what he believes to be Islam. . . .

And you also, the friend of my final moment, who would not be aware of what you were doing. Yes, for you also I wish this "thank you"—and this adieu—to commend you to the God whose face I see in yours.

And may we find each other, happy "good thieves,"
in Paradise, if it pleases God, the Father of us both.
Amen.[14]

Christian de Chergé describes his would-be assassin as the friend of his final moment. There is no anger, no shame, no self-doubt, nor loss of confidence. There is only freedom that has been fuelled by true and unconditional love.

Maybe as we consider the humiliation that the end of this age in the history of our world brings and will bring, we will acknowledge that the only life-giving way we can live is with the courage and freedom of those Trappists, and the Christians in Algeria. I hope we will remember Jeffrey, and how he was able to have a deep

14 Christian de Chergé, "Last Testament," translated by the Monks of Mount Saint Bernard Abbey, Leicester, England. Published in many places in 1996; at the time this book went to press, a copy was available online at http://www.ewtn.com/library/MARY/LASTTEST.htm.

and beautiful relationship with his father. I hope we will consider Pio, who was able to realize that his confidence came from God, and his call was to collaborate with God in his ongoing creation and dream for his life. The same freedom of spirit enabled Christian de Chergé to describe the one who murdered him as his friend.

But how can all of this happen? What is necessary for us to choose freedom after humiliation, to willingly journey from power to poverty? The answers to these questions begin with our hearts. When I speak about our hearts, I am speaking about the core of our being. I am speaking about the engine room of our lives. What is at the core of our being? How are our hearts?

God tells us in the book of the prophet Ezekiel: "I shall give you a new heart, and put a new spirit in you; I shall remove the heart of stone from your bodies and give you a heart of flesh instead" (Ezek. 36:26). Stone or flesh, which would you prefer? For strength, stone is the answer all the time. Stone is hard, durable, solid. Flesh is soft. It is vulnerable. In many ways, it is weak and needs much care. At a time of humiliation, it is understandable

All Things Pass Away 107

to look for what is hard and durable and solid. These are the things that we believe will bring us security and power once more. We believe that if we get what is durable and solid, we will regain our confidence. We will regain our independence. We will be winning again.

So why does God tell us that he is going to take our hearts of stone from our bodies and give us hearts of flesh instead? The person who taunted Jesus from the cross wanted to appear strong and without fear. He wanted to appear confident, not weak. A hard, durable heart is what he wanted. He probably would have wrestled God to keep his stone heart rather than have it replaced with a heart of flesh. It is St. Augustine who said: "It was to strengthen your heart that Jesus suffered and died."

Consider what it is that makes a heart strong. I recently learned something about this the hard way. My father has had heart issues since he was forty-five years old. He is now eighty. At forty-five, he had a triple bypass. When he was fifty-seven, he had another triple bypass. While his first bypass lasted for twelve years, his second lasted for nineteen years. He was very blessed. But, then, in

September 2016, the time came for more intervention to help his heart. With the advances in medicine, instead of open-heart surgery, this time my father got six stents. The following March he got another stent and a pacemaker fitted. Things still were not good for him. My father who loved to walk every morning was not able to. His life was becoming more and more restricted, and he developed heart failure.

In August 2017, my father was admitted to hospital again. He was fitted with a new pacemaker. I saw him a short time after, and he seemed to be fine. However, that night his heart went out of control, and he was brought to intensive care. It was decided then that he needed another procedure. Because he had so much done to his heart over the years, scar tissue had grown over the heart. This was hard tissue growing on a soft organ like a piece of leather being stuck to moving flesh. The scar tissue prohibited the heart from beating properly. The necessary procedure was to burn the scar tissue from his heart. It was by removing the scar tissue that the heart became soft again and free to beat correctly. Dad has been in great health since then.

All Things Pass Away ✥ 109

The truth is that a strong heart is a soft heart. A weak heart is a hard heart. From the words of St. Augustine, then, it is to soften our hearts that Jesus suffered and died. We choose freedom after humiliation when we have the courage to allow God to change our hearts of stone into hearts of flesh. Christian de Chergé lived and died with a strong and soft heart. Pio and Jeffrey have strong and soft hearts. It is the strength that comes from a soft heart that enables us to choose freedom in the face of humiliation. It is the courage that comes from a soft heart that allows us to be pruned, to be vulnerable, because it is only in vulnerability that we can grow. One of the people crucified with Jesus had that courage to be vulnerable. He too died with a heart of flesh—a heart that enabled him to recognize who Jesus was and to acknowledge his need for Jesus. He chose freedom in the face of death, and his freedom brought him to paradise.

Seven
Death

This brings us to the real heart of the matter (no pun intended!): the context in which we live our lives. If the context in which we live is this world only, then our lives will, as we've seen, always be incomplete. If we live our lives both in and beyond this world (which is what we're called to do), then we must talk about death. And how we speak about death, indeed, how we regard our own death that is to come, is very much related to how we live, and whether we are truly alive.

People often try to avoid the reality of death as best they can. We try to ignore it, and even when someone we love dies, in the words of Henri Nouwen, we "bury our dead as if they were still alive."[15] We celebrate their life. We focus on them and not too much on the journey that they have begun in death.

Is death the ultimate failure, the proof that life is incomplete? If so, then, we need to win in this life. We need to beat our competitors. We need to overcome our threats. We need to defeat our enemies. We need to do all this before we die. We need to prove that our lives have been worth living. Living as sisters and brothers doesn't seem to be enough. It could even seem to be a futile exercise if it all ends in death anyway. Is death simply returning to that moment of ultimate vulnerability, which we have tried to avoid all our lives? If so, we avoid it and all discussions about it because we don't want to be vulnerable, and perhaps we panic because we see death as the great unknown.

What exactly happens when we die? We don't know for certain. This goes against so much of what we usually value. We like to know. We like to be in control. We like to have the power.

---

15 Henri Nouwen, *You Are the Beloved* (New York: Convergent Books, 2017), 42.

There is an ultimate poverty and humiliation in death. I saw it as I watched my mother die. She was a bright and fiercely independent lady. As the cancer tore through her body, the poverty that it left in its wake humiliated her. Here was a woman who did so much for so many, and on her deathbed she didn't even have the power to sponge her lips with water.

Sr. Maria Boulding, of course, was able to see dying as a gift. She saw her need as she was dying as a gift. But I struggled to see my mother's need as a gift. I wished, during that time with my mother, that things would all go back to the way they should be. I would have given anything to see my mother independent again and caring for us. That wasn't the way it was going to be.

My mother's death was very peaceful. She took her last breath in this world surrounded by family who were encouraging her to let go and begin the next stage of her journey of life. This was the stage that began when she entered through the doors of death. It was the first stage we felt we couldn't accompany her on. We had accompanied her through her illness, but she had to go on at this stage on her own. When she took her last breath she was gone from us, but to where?

Again, what happens when we die? What happens when we breathe no more in this world? What happens when we can no longer feel the hand that is holding ours in the last moments of life here on earth? What happens?

If death is the end, then life is incomplete. However, if in death we begin a journey to somewhere else, then for those left behind it can be too difficult to think about.

We can't think about our loved ones going somewhere else. We want them to be with us. We want to hold on to them; therefore, we often try to ignore the separation that death inevitably brings.

When we find ourselves in denial about death, or trying to ignore death, it becomes virtually impossible to live our lives in the context of eternal life. We need to live our lives in the context of life that is both now and eternal.

We only see this life clearly (even though one could argue that we really don't see this life all that clearly). But when we only see this life, our vision is restricted, our priorities are transient, and our lives themselves become ultimately futile. There is so much more!

So what about death? Is there any point in talking about it because we believe we know so little about it? I have often heard the phrase, "Nobody has ever come back from the dead." But that's not true. There is one person in history who did die and rise from the dead: Jesus. Did Jesus keep death a mystery, or did he reveal to us what happens when we die? What did Jesus say about death? He said, "I am the resurrection. Anyone who believes in me, even though that person dies, will live, and everyone who lives and believes in me will never die. Do you believe this?" (John 11:25–26)

I was recently with a family at a Mass and time of remembering a husband and father who has been dead for twenty years. One of the family members, Andrew, reflected on what home meant to him. Andrew had traveled from Saudi Arabia to Cork for this Mass and time of remembering. He said:

> It's nice to be home. Home is a comforting voice and a listening ear when the world around you seems unfamiliar and maybe a bit scary. Home is the sound of family, sometimes squabbling, sometimes laughing, but always together. Home is that feeling you get when you return from being away and get into your own bed! Home is a roaring fire when it is wet and windy outside.
>
> Home is sitting on Daddy's knee to watch the back nine of "The Masters" on Sunday or seeing Ireland win a Grand Slam. Home is the 9 o'clock news followed by *The Late Late Show*. Home is going to Mass on Sunday followed by sizzling rashers and sausages on the AGA cooker. Home is Christmas dinners shared, debates

had, and movies watched. Home is being together through good times and bad, for happy moments and disappointments. Home is a collection of memories and feelings that stays with you your whole life no matter where you go. Home is a memory left to me by my father and mother that I will always cherish and use as inspiration for how I build memories for my children.

Look after one another as these are the years that you will carry with you into adulthood and parenthood. No detail of life is too humble or too small. Appreciate it all. It's nice to be home.

The Mass we celebrated was in a small marquee on top of a hill overlooking the ocean. It was very dramatic and beautiful. It was obviously impermanent. A marquee on top of a hill beside the sea on the southern coast of Ireland reveals either great faith or foolishness! However, we were blessed that the usual wind didn't blow that day. In the midst of our physical impermanence, when Andrew started to reflect on home, he painted a picture of permanence and warmth and love. It enabled us to turn back the clock to an idyllic time of security, peace, and love. Home was the place without stress where everything stayed the same and we felt total belonging. It was our place. A safe place. It was a permanent sanctuary. Having a wonderful childhood home is one of the greatest blessings a child can receive.

In many respects, the reality of death, which reveals the vulnerability and fragility of life, is what can destroy home. The permanence, the security, the love does not come from the bricks and mortar. These things come from the people in the home—particularly the parents. When parents die, "home" can die too. This often causes another bereavement. Death can make reflecting on home very difficult and painful. We remember (and want to remember) a time past when people were together, and that time is no more.

It is St. Paul who makes one of the most wonderful declarations about death. He says: "For us, our homeland is in heaven" (Phil. 3:20). What does it mean if heaven is our home—our eternal home? It means that heaven is the place of ultimate security, of peace, of belonging, of love. It is where we want to go back to when we are away and, as Andrew reminded us, "get into your own bed."

Yet we know from our reflection on our childhood home that it is not the house that makes the home. It is the people there. What makes heaven home is the fact that God is there. Jesus is there. This is the comforting reality that Jesus reveals to the apostles when he says: "Do not let your hearts be troubled. Trust in God still, and trust in me. There are many rooms in my Father's house; if there were not, I should have told you. I am going now to prepare a place for you, and after I have gone and prepared you a place, I shall return to take you with me; so that where I am you may be too" (John 14:1–4). Jesus goes to prepare a place at home in heaven for us. And when he does that, he doesn't simply give us the keys and send us on our own. No! Jesus comes to take us with him so that we can be together with him in heaven. Being at home is being with Jesus. Jesus is Home.

When we die, we begin the final stage of our journey home, if that is what we choose.

The funeral liturgy of the Catholic Church reveals the journey from life to death so profoundly, so beautifully, and with so much life. The use of holy water in the liturgy marries the beginning of our earthly life to our homeland in heaven. When the body of the one who has died arrives at the church door, it is sprinkled with holy water, and the minister says: "In the waters of baptism our loved one died with Christ and rose with him to new life. May he/she share with him now eternal glory." In other words, when the one who has died was baptized, his or her life was placed in the context of eternal life.

The reality that we live in eternal life is also revealed when the body is placed before the altar and the white funeral pall engulfs the body. This pall reflects the white garment that was placed on the one who has died when they were baptized. After a person is baptized, as the white garment is placed on them, the minister of the sacrament says: "You have become a new creation and have clothed yourself in Christ. See in this white garment the outward sign of your Christian dignity. With your family and friends bring that dignity unstained into the everlasting life of heaven."

The journey of life has gone from the white garment at Baptism to the white pall at the funeral. The symbolism of the white garment and the white pall is very powerful. It is the symbol of belonging—of belonging to God. The garment and the pall could be compared to a towel. I have a vivid memory of being bathed as a young child. At the end of the bath, when I stood up I was always freezing. I was leaving the warm water and standing in what felt like very cold air. Then my mother hugged me with a big bath towel that had been on the radiator. The warmth and the security and the love were wonderful. When we are baptized, we are wrapped in the white garment by Jesus. When we die, if we choose, we are wrapped in that garment again.

In many ways, our time in this earth is a time spent between leaving home and returning home. Before we are born into this world, we already exist in God. When we die, we can go home to God to the "everlasting life of heaven." This is revealed to us in the book of the prophet Jeremiah when God says: "Before I formed you in the womb I knew you; before you came to birth I consecrated you" (Jer. 1:5). So the moment of death can be the moment of return. We return to the home we came from.

The journey that continues in death, the journey home, is a dramatic journey that is revealed in many of the prayers used in the funeral liturgy. One of the prayers that can be used when a person's body is being carried into the Church is this one:

> May Christ, who was crucified for your sake, free you from torments; may Christ, who died for you, deliver you from eternal death; may Christ the son of the living God, set you down in the fresh beauty of his paradise and may he, the Good Shepherd, claim you as one of his flock; may he forgive you all your sins and grant you a place among the elect at his own right hand. There may you ever behold your Redeemer face to face and ever stand before him enraptured by the beauty of Truth itself and, placed in the ranks of

the blessed, may you delight in the vision of God for ever and ever.

There is such drama in this prayer. Jesus is the one who carries you in paradise. He gently sets you down in the "fresh beauty." There is a late spring, early summer feel about his meadow in paradise. There is God in the midst of everybody present, holding out his right hand to you to keep you close to him. I can see me as the child of God looking up into God's face—a beautiful, gentle, compassionate, forgiving, and loving face. Eternity is delighting in that moment.

The prayers in the funeral liturgy continue to reveal what brings us to that moment. These are action-filled prayers. When a person's body is being sprinkled again with holy water and incensed during the final commendation, we pray the Song of Farewell. The response to this song is: "Receive his/her soul and present him/her to God the Most High." This reveals that there are more people involved in our journey back home to God. Others will be there to present us to God. Jesus will be there. He is setting us down in the fresh beauty of paradise. In the first verse of the Song of Farewell, others are asked to be involved, too, in this journey home. We pray, "Saints of God, come to his/her aid! Hasten to meet him/her, angels of the Lord!" Everybody in heaven is part of the welcoming committee that brings us home to Jesus, back home to God. There is great excitement in heaven at our return home.

When we come face-to-face with God, what happens? What happens when we look up into the beautiful, gentle, compassionate, forgiving, and loving face of God? Perhaps Jean Vanier can help us answer this question. When he was asked what happens when we die, he replied:

When you die, you fall asleep. And you wake up, and there's a very gentle peace. You feel well. And then you discover the face of God coming through that "wellness." Of course, we are outside time, so it's not sequential. Seeing Jesus' face, we suddenly have a feeling of having hurt him—we realize we could have done much better, we've done wrong. We are not being judged, we judge ourselves. But then comes the realisation that we are loved just as we are, in our darkness. So there's a meeting with God, who loves us in our poverty—and this we can hardly believe. That meeting brings an immense desire to be closer. That desire becomes a place of desire—I think of Purgatory as "the place of desire"—and it's painful. When you have desire and not the object of desire, it's very painful. But then the desire augments, and consequently the pain augments, until there is a moment of explosion, and then we're in communion with God.[16]

When we die, if we choose, we can see God face-to-face forever. It is an eternal moment of unimaginable joy. We are at home, safe, secure, enfolded in love and peace.

16 Jean Vanier, interview with Ruth Gledhill, *The Tablet* (London, UK), November 7, 2017.

We are back in our own bed with Jesus there to comfort us. The question that begs to be answered is, Why do we fear this reality? Why are we afraid to go home? Why do we ignore the truth that we are on a journey home every day we live in this world?

One of the thieves crucified with Jesus realized there was more to life than this world. That is why he could say to Jesus, "Remember me when you get home." The other thief was full of fear because he couldn't see beyond this world. He was stuck. One was free because he saw this life in the context of the kingdom of heaven; it gave him the patience to wait for Jesus to remember him when he got home. He did not expect his situation to be fixed immediately.

My being ordained, while my mother was dying, only made sense if we are all on the journey back home. Our heavenly home gives us the context in which to live here on earth. The power, the poverty, the humiliation, the pyramid are all only earthly realities. The body of Christ, our vulnerability—these are eternal. Therefore, they are what really matters.

Eight
For the Road Home

While reflecting on death, the journey home to God, I used the phrase "if you choose" a number of times. We have a choice to go home to heaven.

We have a choice to see God face-to-face. It is God's desire that we do go home to him, but he will never force us. He has given us the map to get home, but all roads don't lead home. How do we access and read the map that leads us home? The prophet Jeremiah offers us an answer to this question. God, speaking about his people, says: "Deep within them I will plant my Law, writing it on their hearts" (Jer. 31:33). Just think about that—the Law of God is written on the heart of each one of us, on the soft heart of each one of us. What God is telling us is that in our hearts is the road map to heaven.

What does that mean? I think that it means two things. The first is that we naturally know the way to heaven. We naturally know how not to hurt Jesus, how to live well, and to do what is right and avoid doing what is wrong. You can see this in children. They know right from wrong at such an early age. That doesn't mean they won't do what is wrong, but if they do, they will always look round to see if they are going to be caught! As we grow older, we seem to try to complicate and confuse things. We try to create gray areas. We try to justify our wrong actions. Most of the time we are just fooling ourselves. We are allowing scar tissue to harden our hearts and cover where God has written.

Our hearts, which could also be called the places of our consciences, are that sacred sanctuary within each one of us where we are at one with God. It is the place in our lives where we read God's writing. In that place, we get the answer to what is right and what is wrong. In that place, we get the road map to heaven. How do we get that answer? How do we read that answer in our hearts? This brings me to the second thing.

We need help to read what God writes in our hearts—in our place of conscience. It is very difficult to get home on our own. Like Sr. Maria Boulding, as she approached her death, we have the gift of our need in trying to read what God has written on our hearts. Just like those around Sr. Maria responded to her need, Jesus responds to our need. In his response, Jesus gives us the gift of his body. In his body, we find the help we need.

Help also comes through prayer, through hearing the words of Jesus in the Gospel, through the teaching of the Church, through celebrating all of the sacraments. All these things help us to read what is written by God in our hearts, in our conscience. All these things help us find and follow the road map to home through places of poverty and humiliation, always traveling in the reality of our vulnerability. Because of that vulnerability we need great freedom to travel home. We need great patience too. We need to be able to wait.

Our need for freedom to travel the road home, which could be described as a fruit of patience, is revealed in the story of two people on the road to Emmaus (see Lk. 24:13–35).

Jesus had died. The hope of those two people on the road was in the past tense. They were imprisoned by their disappointment, and they didn't have the patience to wait. They walked on to nowhere. They didn't wait for the map to get home. Waiting and patience are integral parts of life—elements of our journey to freedom, which is our journey to heaven.

In the world of the instant, how do we learn to be patient? How can we value waiting? Why should we need to be patient and wait? Can God not do everything now? If being at home in heaven is so good, why can we not be there now?

To be patient is to live your life according to somebody else's clock. It is living your life in somebody else's rhythm that is not your own. That can be a real challenge. We like things done in our time, and we don't like waiting. We like things when it suits us, and it is harder when we have to suit others.

I am naturally impatient! In the summer of 1994 I worked for a month in a hospice. I sat with people who were dying. I also sat with their families. I brought Holy Communion to people. For the most part I did well. I was present to people. But one day I was asked to feed a man who was dying with cancer. This elderly man was very weak. He couldn't lift the food to his mouth. I fed him custard. When he took a spoonful of custard into this mouth, it took him a long time to swallow it. After a short while, I became intensely impatient. I was awful. I kept saying, "Another spoonful now," hoping he would open his mouth and we'd get the bowl finished.

A nurse was passing the ward while I was doing this. She heard me and came in and asked that I didn't say anything and just wait until the man was ready for his next spoonful. I was ashamed at my impatience. I really struggled to enter into the old man's rhythm. It can be difficult to wait.

This is why examples of patient people can be so humbling to watch. I think of children caring for an elderly parent. They eat at the speed they eat. They walk at the speed they walk, and they allow them to take the time they need to remember and to say what they want to say. They don't run on ahead, or leave them behind. They give in and surrender to a different rhythm. I found that difficult and frustrating, but it is beautiful to witness. Maybe that is our question for life: in whose rhythm do we live our lives?

There is a powerful line in the Gospel of Luke where Jesus says, "Happy is the man who does not lose faith in me" (7:23) It almost sounds as if Jesus expects that we won't have patience. We won't wait. We will lose faith because we think that Jesus is taking too long. This reveals the humility of Jesus—to be surprised that people keep faith in him. If they do, they are blessed. Patience with Jesus brings blessing.

Jesus never tells us that anything is going to be instant or even quick. This is a point made clearly in the Letter of St. James. James explicitly tells us to be patient. He says: "Think of the farmer: how patiently he waits for the precious fruits of the ground until it has the autumn rains and the spring rains! You too have to be patient" (Jas. 5:7–8)

We are not called to be in a place of inactivity where nothing happens. Life in this world is not like sitting in a waiting room. This would drive us mad! Our waiting—our call to be patient—is a call to surrender the rhythm we want for our lives and accept the rhythm of God's life. Patience allows us to enter the rhythm of God. When we do that, we are more aware as we live our lives. It enables us to connect with our hearts, our consciences, and to find, read, and follow the road map to heaven.

Conclusion

I was talking to a friend recently about God. I asked him where was God in his life. He hesitated at first. But I am quite persistent in my questioning, and so I kept pushing and pushing. Eventually he arrived at an image, and the image was that he was driving the car and God was in the passenger seat. God was there for advice, for directions, and for company.

I love this image! Our lives are always in motion, and God is there right beside us. We bring God with us wherever we are going. What is better than driving along the journey of your life with God sitting beside you? Let God do the driving.

When God is driving, it lifts so much of the pressure of life. God can't crash! When God is in the driving seat, we are also safe. But when God is driving, we can look. We can see the beauty of creation. We can see the beauty of the body of Christ where we all belong. When God is driving, no matter what terrain we have to go through, no matter what suffering we have to endure, no matter what poverty or humiliation, we are safe. When God is driving, we don't need to have any fear, because we are being driven home, "back to our own bed."

However, on the journey home we would be wrong to think that when God is driving we can simply recline the seat and rest. God regularly stops the car and asks us to get out and do something with him, or for him. This is what Jesus did. Jesus tells us: "I have come from heaven, not to do my own will, but to do the will of the one who sent me" (John 6:38). We are not our own property. We have been entrusted to do the will of God. We have been entrusted to do the definite service that God has created us to do. It is our mission, and it is unique to each one of us.

The end result will be arriving back home. Then, rather than death revealing the incompleteness of life, death is what makes life complete. Rather than death being the ultimate failure, death becomes, in fact, the ultimate homecoming. When we see death as the front door of our home, we are freed to allow God to drive us home. Pope Francis has said: "The free man is not afraid of time: he lets God do the work. He allows God to take his time. The free man is patient."[17]

In the car with God, there is no ring road around Calvary. But when we allow God to drive, we can be confident that we won't be ending our journey on Calvary. John, the Beloved Disciple, knew that his journey wouldn't end at the Calvary of powerlessness. The body of Christ, the Church, knows that her journey won't end at the Calvary of abuse. Christian de Chergé knew his journey wouldn't end at the Calvary of his murder. Jeffrey knew that his journey wouldn't end at the Calvary of his father's abuse. Pio knew that his journey wouldn't end at the Calvary of

---

17 Pope Francis, homily preached in Santa Marta, April 13, 2018.

his bankruptcy. I knew that my journey wouldn't end at the Calvary of my mother's death. That is why I could be ordained and why I could be celibate.

Because our lives don't end in this world, Calvary does not have to have the last word. Because our lives end back at home with God in heaven, no single event in this world can fully define us. We cannot be defined only by our power or our poverty or our humiliation or indeed our freedom. Our lives are greater than any or all of these.

When I was young, my family visited Donegal Town once a year in the summer. For a number of years, every day that we visited the sun shone. Because of this, my sister firmly believed that it never rained in Donegal Town! The fact is that it didn't rain on the one day per year that we visited for about four years running. That is only four days altogether. It could have rained every other day. We just weren't there to see it.

When we take one moment of our lives out of context, we usually reach the wrong conclusion that doesn't reflect reality. When we live life out of context, we usually reach the wrong conclusion that doesn't reflect reality either. When we live life in the context of Home, of Jesus, we reach the right conclusion, and we can face reality but not be held captive by any single moment of it. We reach the right conclusion because we are faithful to the road map that leads us home when we allow God to drive.

Every road doesn't lead us home, but there is a road from everywhere that will bring us home to God. When we discover that road and use the map and allow God to drive, we can only reply as St. Peter replied when Jesus asked the apostles, "'What about you, do you want to go away too?' Peter said, 'Lord, who shall we go to? You have the message of eternal life and we believe'" (John 6:67–69).

Acknowledgments

Thank you to Jon Sweeney and all at Paraclete Press for their encouragement and patience and for publishing this book.

Thank you to Timothy Shriver for writing the foreword. I deeply appreciate his kindness and his generosity.

Thank you to all those who helped me to write this book and who inspired me by their faith and their love, especially Pio and Jeffrey.

Thank you also to my friend Jean Vanier who supported me so much in writing this book and named the chapters. He agreed to write the afterword but illness and death intervened. As I witnessed his final illness and death what he said about dying in 2017 he believed to the end. He acknowledged, when he struggled to talk and was unable to eat or drink and was confined to his bed, that he was in the place of desire. I have no doubt that when he breathed his last breath in this world it was the moment of explosion when he was in communion with God. May he live for ever in the joy of seeing God face to face and from there may he intercede for us all.

About Paraclete Press

Who We Are

As the publishing arm of the Community of Jesus, Paraclete Press presents a full expression of Christian belief and practice—from Catholic to Evangelical, from Protestant to Orthodox, reflecting the ecumenical charism of the Community and its dedication to sacred music, the fine arts, and the written word. We publish books, recordings, sheet music, and video/DVDs that nourish the vibrant life of the church and its people.

What We Are Doing

Books | PARACLETE PRESS BOOKS show the richness and depth of what it means to be Christian. While Benedictine spirituality is at the heart of who we are and all that we do, our books reflect the Christian experience across many cultures, time periods, and houses of worship.

We have many series, including *Paraclete Essentials; Paraclete Fiction; Paraclete Poetry; Paraclete Giants;* and for children and adults, *All God's Creatures*, books about animals and faith; and *San Damiano Books*, focusing on Franciscan spirituality. Others include *Voices from the Monastery* (men and women monastics writing about living a spiritual life today), *Active Prayer*, and new for young readers: *The Pope's Cat*. We also specialize in gift books for children on the occasions of Baptism and First Communion, as well as other important times in a child's life, and books that bring creativity and liveliness to any adult spiritual life.

The Mount Tabor Books series focuses on the arts and literature as well as liturgical worship and spirituality; it was created in conjunction with the Mount Tabor Ecumenical Centre for Art and Spirituality in Barga, Italy.

Music | THE PARACLETE RECORDINGS label represents the internationally acclaimed choir *Gloriæ Dei Cantores*, the *Gloriæ Dei Cantores Schola*, and the other instrumental artists of the *Arts Empowering Life Foundation*.

Paraclete Press is the exclusive North American distributor for the Gregorian chant recordings from St. Peter's Abbey in Solesmes, France. Paraclete also carries all of the Solesmes chant publications for Mass and the Divine Office, as well as their academic research publications.

In addition, PARACLETE PRESS SHEET MUSIC publishes the work of today's finest composers of sacred choral music, annually reviewing over 1,000 works and releasing between 40 and 60 works for both choir and organ.

Video | Our video/DVDs offer spiritual help, healing, and biblical guidance for a broad range of life issues including grief and loss, marriage, forgiveness, facing death, understanding suicide, bullying, addictions, Alzheimer's, and Christian formation.

Learn more about us at our website:
www.paracletepress.com,
or call us toll-free at 1-800-451-5006.

SCAN TO READ MORE

You may also be interested in . . .

Freedom and Forgiveness:
A Fresh Look at the Sacrament of Reconciliation
Fr. Paul Farren
Preface by Catherine Dooley, OP,
Afterword by Jean Vanier
ISBN 978-1-61261-498-4 | $9.99 | Trade paperback

The Light of Forgiveness:
The Sacrament of Reconciliation for Teens
Fr. Paul Farren
ISBN 978-1-61261-758-9 | $9.99 | Trade paperback

"Father Paul's new book is a beautiful invitation
into the sacrament of reconciliation, perhaps the
most misunderstood sacrament in the church.
With his clear, helpful and accessible writing,
Freedom and Forgiveness reminds the reader that the
sacrament is about not how bad you are,
but about how good God is."
—JAMES MARTIN, SJ

We Need Each Other
Responding to God's Call to Live Together
Jean Vanier
ISBN 978-1-64060-450-6 | $14.99 | Trade paperback

"Jean Vanier brings you in touch with a place
inside yourself that few people have reached."
—HENRI J. M. NOUWEN

Available at bookstores
Paraclete Press
1-800-451-5006
www.paracletepress.com